REFERENCING
FOR
GENEALOGISTS

SOURCES
AND
CITATION

IAN G. MACDONALD

T0333432

The
History
Press

First published 2018

The History Press
The Mill, Brimscombe Port
Stroud, Gloucestershire, GL5 2QG
www.thehistorypress.co.uk

British Library Cataloguing in Publication Data.
A catalogue record for this book is available from the British Library.

ISBN 978 0 7509 8688 5

Typesetting and origination by The History Press
Printed and bound by TJ International Ltd, Padstow, Cornwall

Contents

Foreword 5

The Strathclyde experience 5

The background to this work 5

Contributors and collaborators 6

1 **INTRODUCTION** 7

Quality in genealogical investigation:
why does all this matter? 7

What do we mean by sources? 7

Primary and secondary sources 8

A trail to follow for those who come after 9

What exactly is 'referencing' or 'citation'? 10

How far can you go with material from
others? 11

The nature of evidence 13

Limits to evidence 15

Standards of acceptability in genealogy 16

The digital revolution 17

2 **THE MATERIALS WE USE AND THE
PLACES WE FIND THEM** 18

The physical 18

The digital: written, spoken, video 19

3 **CREATING INDIVIDUAL
REFERENCES: PRINCIPLES** 20

Key elements and guidelines 20

Characterising the source material 21

Specifying the location 21

Dealing with versions 22

Capturing the references 23

4 **THE 'HARVARD' STYLE** 24

Origin; lack of a standard 24

Publishers' tastes 25

Some published versions 25

5 **USING OUR 'HARVARD' IN THE
DIGITAL AGE** 27

URL/web address guidelines 27

6 **USING 'HARVARD' STYLE FOR
SECONDARY SOURCES** 30

Referencing a monograph 30

Referencing a monograph within a series 37

Referencing a chapter in a book 38

Referencing a dictionary or
encyclopaedia entry 39

Referencing a biographical or alumnus entry 40

Referencing a journal paper or magazine
article 43

Referencing a conference paper 45

Referencing an unpublished thesis
or dissertation 46

Referencing an archived letter 47

7 **CLOUD SOURCING** 49

Referencing an item of personal e-mail 49

Referencing an item read on an electronic
mail discussion list or forum 50

Referencing an item from an online blog
or vlog 50

Referencing a web page 51

Referencing information found using an
e-book reader 53

8 **REFERENCING FOR GENEALOGICAL
AND ARCHIVAL SOURCES** 55

Some theoretical background 55

Genealogical sources and their classification 56

Major source categories 57

Source types 58

Sources for sources 60

Records and indexes 60
Belt and braces 61
General structure for genealogical references 61

9 **NOMINAL RECORDS** 63
Referencing BMD records 63
Referencing census returns 74
Referencing electoral listings 80
Referencing directories and professional lists 82
Referencing membership lists 84
Referencing service records 86
Referencing testamentary records 89
Referencing monumental inscriptions 91
Referencing newspaper announcements
    and obituaries 94
Referencing grants of arms 95

10 **MATERIAL RECORDS** 97
Land and buildings 97
Referencing tithe maps and apportionments 98
Referencing manorial records 99
Referencing inquisitions post mortem 100
Referencing sasines 101
Referencing retours 102
Referencing Scottish royal charters 103
Referencing valuation rolls 104
Referencing Griffith's valuations 105
Personal possessions 105
Intellectual property 107

11 **PROCEDURAL RECORDS** 108
Referencing travel records 108
Referencing court proceedings 110
Referencing admission registers 112
Referencing prison registers 113
Referencing poor relief records 114
Referencing taxation records 115

12 **OTHER PRIMARY RECORDS:**
   GUIDELINES 117
Referencing newspaper articles 119
Referencing official reports 120
Referencing legislation 121
Referencing ephemera 123
Referencing a letter, conversation
    or private correspondence 124

13 **IMAGES** 125

14 **MAPS** 127

15 **USING THE REFERENCING PRINCIPLES**
   IN YOUR OWN WRITING 129
Footnotes and endnotes 129
Bibliographies 130

16 **WORKING WITH SOFTWARE** 133
Bibliographical referencing software 133
Genealogical software 133

17 **FUTURE CITATION** 135
Life's audit trail 135
An expanding world of administrative
    records 136
Mining social media? 136
Linking to DNA analyses? 137

18 **ENDPOINT: OR A NEW BEGINNING** 139

Bibliography 140
Notes 142
Index 143

Foreword

Genealogy is little more than anecdote when the sources for facts are not cited and where clear references to sources are not given. That may be a harsh judgement, but in a world awash with poor genealogy it is a call for raising standards.

This book is about making your work better, more credible, more useful and easier to communicate to all those who may be interested in it, and in what you have achieved and wish to say.

Referencing may seem a bit daunting at first but, like so many things, it is straightforward once you get used to it. The book concentrates on general principles and offers many examples to illuminate what is going on. As a bonus, there are many sources cited in the examples that are valuable to every genealogical researcher, and some may take your investigations off on new paths.

The Strathclyde experience

This book has its origins in, and takes its inspiration from, things initiated not so long ago in Scotland that, themselves, are part of a continuing effort to raise standards in genealogical practice.

The University of Strathclyde launched its first courses in postgraduate-level genealogical studies in 2005. These were taught on campus in Glasgow and made available online. A switch to complete online delivery and tuition soon followed. The initial offering of a postgraduate certificate was immediately followed by a postgraduate diploma and soon could be followed by a year of supervised research leading to the degree of Master of Science in genealogical studies – the first of its kind in the world.

The first students graduated with their diplomas in 2008 and with MSc degrees in 2010. The emergence of these qualified genealogists marked a step change in genealogical practice, not just in the UK but around the world in the many other countries where Strathclyde's online students are based.

The background to this work

From the outset, Strathclyde courses insisted on a high quality of delivery from students that would build on the prior experience they all possessed. So, as part of the disciplined, systematic approach demanded of them in their investigative work they

5

were expected to provide clear identification of all sources used in reaching their genealogical conclusions.

Guidance was provided to them in how to cite these sources and on how to format references. That guidance has been improved and enhanced over the years to make it ever more suited to good genealogical practice. Until now the material has been available only to students, but there has been a growing recognition that it could be of value to a wider audience.

For that wider audience, the guidance and explanation has been expanded much further to create this small book in the hope that it will be of service to the genealogical community.

The book does view sources and referencing from a UK perspective. However, it assumes that immigration and emigration, and families scattered worldwide, are an integral part of that perspective. Sources from many parts of the world, from wherever a family has spread to, must therefore be used and cited in support of genealogical conclusions. A consistently clear way of referring to these sources is thus essential to enable good communication among practitioners. The approach in this book is sufficiently general to be valuable to anyone from outside the UK, particularly those with a link to the UK. That being said, the book's focus is also primarily on sources from the English-speaking world.

Contributors and collaborators

Ian Macdonald has prepared this book for publication. However, it has its origins in material prepared by Bruce Durie and Graham Holton, the initiators of the Strathclyde courses, and has been enhanced greatly over subsequent years by Tahitia McCabe and other members of the Strathclyde tutor team.

Some examples have been gleaned from the work of students. These citations have not themselves been cited – that all felt too incestuous – and, in any case, they have mostly been adapted. Lessons too have been learned by observing students struggle with some formats so, if this book makes things seem more straightforward, then thanks must be offered to all.

Other support has been given by members of the Register of Qualified Genealogists (www.qualifiedgenealogists.org), an exceptional group of professionals.

Various examples relate to Mewburns, a family that simply happens to have been studied in detail. More on them can be found at www.mewburn.one-name.net.

Some wording remains from the Strathclyde guidelines along with occasional examples. I am grateful to the University of Strathclyde for permission to incorporate these elements.

1

Introduction

Quality in genealogical investigation: why does all this matter?

Findings need to be communicable. We take this to be a fundamental principle. If findings cannot be shared they have no value. This book is not for the genealogical hermit whose work is to follow them to the grave.

Genealogists gather data relating to people who lived in the past and they use that data to infer things about those people's lives and, most importantly, to infer familial linkages between them. Notions of ancestry or descent are developed. Whether or not these notions are correct and the linkages are accurately made are central to good genealogy – by which we mean reliable genealogy. Reliable genealogy is genealogy that can be replicated. The quality of the work is assured when others can reach the same point, and come to the same conclusions, by using the same information sources.

Reliable conclusions depend on reliable data. The old GIGO acronym – garbage in garbage out – beloved of practitioners in information technology, applies equally to genealogy. We need to be able to convince others that the data is reliable and that there is therefore a sound basis for conclusions. Good genealogy revolves around ways of establishing how good the data is. It proceeds in steps, where logic is applied to the discovered data to determine causal linkages. If the data is at any point unreliable, the logic fails and can produce false or misleading conclusions.

Central to any good investigation is, therefore, an appreciation of where the data came from – the source – because, by knowing where it came from, any other investigator can re-examine it and re-establish conclusions reached by others. Equally importantly, they may be able to re-interpret those conclusions by introducing newly found material. By providing references to sources, so indicating where the information can be found, a transparency is added to any investigation. That transparency offers an assurance of quality because all assertions made can always be checked.

What do we mean by sources?

Quite simply, a source is a place where data is found and from which relevant information is gleaned. It is some form of record in the broadest sense, whether it be on paper, carved in stone or in the form of a SNP[1] found in DNA analysis.

Data consists of values in the record. Of themselves the values convey no meaning until placed in a defined context – at which point they become information.

03Apr1851 is data. It is just a string of numbers and letters and tells us nothing. We may think it is a date, but that is just an assumption based on poor evidence (we infer that from the format, but we might be more reluctant to accept it as a date if, for example, the data were 3Ap8 – and indeed a record from the year 8 would be remarkable). That data becomes information only when it is in a field headed 'Birth Date in day-month-year format', so that some meaning is assigned to it. It then becomes useful information to the genealogist, and becomes all the more so when it is concatenated with a 'Name' like Jemima Jones.

Sources, then, are forms of record with data positioned in meaningful contexts. Genealogy builds from its sources – depending on how reliable they are. Typically, we try to categorise sources to indicate something about their possible reliability.

Primary and secondary sources

A **primary** source is a document or physical object which was (usually) created either during or close to the event or time-period in question. It can be an original, first-hand account of an event or time-period. Some types of primary sources include:

- Original documents: diaries, family bibles, birth certificates, census records, letters, interviews, news film footage, autobiographies, government legislation, international standards and many more;
- Creative works: poetry, drama, novels, music, art;
- Science: reports of scientific discoveries, social and political science research results, results of clinical trials, results from a DNA analysis;
- Relics or artefacts: pottery, furniture, clothing, buildings.

Primary sources provide us with data or raw facts that, placed in context, become information we can use to build a picture of a person's life, or that of a family. Typically, the data requires close examination to determine its exact nature and significance. Only then can the facts be used with confidence, collectively, to provide an interpretation of circumstances that can serve as a history.

Examples of primary sources include:

- Newspaper or magazine articles which are factual accounts of events of the time;
- Diaries such as *The Diary of Anne Frank*;
- Government Acts such as the Education (Scotland) Act of 1872;
- A journal article reporting new research or findings;
- Photographs by Diane Arbus of migrants to California;
- A 1911 English census householder return [these were filled in by the householder; earlier ones were filled in by an official];
- The 2013 United Arab Emirates State Visit Programme at the official UK royal website *The home of the Royal Family*: https://www.royal.uk/united-arab-emirates-state-visit-programme;

- A blog item reporting on the events of the uprising in Cairo in 2013 as they occurred;
- A Twitter entry commenting on a current event in an individual's life.

Things are not always as clear cut as this might suggest. There are many types of record that are almost primary; primary-ish, if you like. Many of these get termed 'derived primary'. A derived primary source is a source based on a primary source but with a level of intermediation (when someone else has had a hand in it); for example, a transcription of a census record, a Bishop's Transcript of a parish record, or an abstract of a will. We will look at these more closely a little later when dealing with the nature of evidence.

Secondary sources are quite different. Whenever we read around a subject and gather background information most of the materials we use, like books or journal articles, will be secondary sources. A secondary source interprets and analyses primary sources. It may be based on primary sources, other secondary sources or a mixture of the two. Secondary sources are one or more steps removed from the event and are often written at a date later than the events being described. However, secondary sources may present pictures, quotes or graphics from primary sources.

Examples of secondary sources include:

- A journal or magazine article which interprets or reviews previous findings or work;
- A history book such as *The Highland Clearances* by John Prebble;
- Encyclopaedias or dictionaries such as the *Oxford Dictionary of National Biography;*
- A newspaper article written in 1980 about the long-term economic effects of the First World War;
- A website entry such as the Henry VIII portion of the official UK royal website *The home of the Royal Family*: https://www.royal.uk/search?tags[0]=Henry%20VIII.

It is typical of a secondary source that the author has put a personal stamp on the material presented. The secondary source is an individual view of things, however authoritative or canonical it is intended to be. All writing about history is secondary.

A trail to follow for those who come after

It is a good discipline to record details about your sources as you use them. These details can include names of the authors, the title of a website or book, the URL of a website and the date the item was published. The details needed for different sources vary, so please check the sections on secondary and primary sources below. Noting and writing down these details as you make use of sources can save many unhappy hours spent 're-finding' source material in order to create your references.

When you write any form of family history, or even just make a family tree available online, you should always aim to allow your readers to go back and check the details for themselves. Their perspective and interests will be a little different. They may be looking for links to other families and historical events; they may have access to new data that permits an altered interpretation. The trail that you leave (an audit trail, if you want to be technical) needs to show others who follow exactly where you found your facts. The clues you leave are the references you cite. The reference, therefore, must be clear and unambiguous so that the trail can be retraced.

What exactly is 'referencing' or 'citation'?

Referencing is quite simply providing details of where you found your information. Typically, it is a matter of saying what the source is, where it can be found and, possibly, where within it the specific information lies.

Citation takes place within your text and provides a pointer to the reference for the source you have made use of. You are placing a marker to acknowledge your use, at that point, of an idea or wording gleaned from elsewhere.

As a general guide:

- If you draw on someone else's opinion, facts, or generalisations, you must offer a reference to that writer and his/her work and provide a citation for it; or
- If you use his or her words directly, use quotation marks around that quote within your work and, again, provide a citation.

This simply lets the reader know you are presenting information you have found and indicates where it has come from and where they can find it. It is also a courtesy to the author to acknowledge their contribution to the general understanding of things. So, you must cite and give references for:

- Assertions of fact that cannot be presumed to be common knowledge;
- Direct quotations or paraphrases of other writers;
- Opinions and generalisations derived directly from other writers; and
- Tables and diagrams.

There are three interlocking parts to citing and referencing within your writing:

1. Indicating your use of a quote or information from another source within your work – i.e. citing.
2. Creating individual references for each source you've cited within your work.

3. Linking the citation of a quote and/or information within your work (from point 1), through the use of a superscript number, to the corresponding individual reference (that you created as point 2) in either the footnotes that come at the bottom of the page of text on which the quote or data appears or in endnotes collected at the end of the whole document.

Each of these parts will be described individually below, but remember that this is an interlocking system and no part can stand alone.

How far can you go with material from others?

Safely using quotes and information from other sources

Direct quotes from another's work need to be placed within quotation marks, for example:

> In her bestselling history of Scotland from 1999, Dr Clancy stated, "All the best boiled sweets come from Dundee and were first created during the mid-1850s."[13] Clearly this is a hotly disputed claim and many have responded to her statement.

As we've said, assertions of fact that cannot be presumed to be common knowledge (in the context of genealogical work, this includes the birth, marriage, death, occupational and other information you will be reporting), paraphrases of other writers, generalisations and opinions derived directly from other writers, and tables and diagrams created by someone other than yourself, should be cited and given references. For example:

> In 1845, there were three brothers in Glasgow, the Sullivans, making a hard sweet from molasses, which was advertised fortnightly in the *Glasgow Crier*.[14] It can be argued that this candy could be seen to be a boiled sweet and thus a forerunner of the infamous Dundee species.

The information on the Sullivans and their molasses sweet was taken directly from a fictitious article in a journal written by one Dr McBrien of Western Kentucky University and thus needs to have a reference created for it.

For example, in the footnotes section that comes at the bottom of the page on which the information or quote appears, a reference for the information cited by the superscript 14 might appear like this:

14 McBrien, Angela. 2008. First boilings or the sticky history of sweets in Scotland. *History notes*. 4(13). p. 45.

Note that the page number from which the quote was taken is given at the end of the reference. This enables the reader to find the exact place from where the quote or information comes rather than having to read through the entire work. This is very important to the reader!

When in doubt, create a reference for the information used; it is better to over-cite and reference from the outset rather than leave your reader wondering where you found a piece of information. This is particularly important in an academic setting to eliminate any question of plagiarism.

Plagiarism

Citation and referencing are an antidote to plagiarism. Plagiarism, quite simply, is passing off other people's work as your own. Most often that is done by copying text and incorporating it into some published work of yours without acknowledging the source. It can also be done by using someone else's idea – again without acknowledgement.

Plagiarism is unacceptable because it is a form of theft – in this case of intellectual property. Naturally, we are all influenced by other people's ideas and published material. The right thing to do though is to acknowledge such influences and cite references to the sources.

Our ideas and understanding grow within the context of other materials and thoughts that we have referred to and have become familiar with. Our conclusions emerge from the ways we have analysed that information so it is proper to let others appreciate how we got to those conclusions.

We do not pursue this to absurd levels. We do not cite all conversations with influential friends or every book we read during our school days. We do cite material we have studied and taken note of when preparing a piece of genealogical work or a family history.

Here are examples of the kinds of things that can constitute plagiarism:

- Inclusion of phrases or ideas from another's work without the use of quotation marks and appropriate acknowledgement of the source;
- Summarising somebody else's work without acknowledgement;
- Paraphrasing somebody else's work by changing a few words or altering the order of presentation without acknowledgement;
- Copying somebody else's work;
- Using somebody else's ideas, theories or opinions without acknowledgement, or presenting work which is substantially somebody else's ideas as one's own;
- Collusion or the representation of a piece of group-work as the work of a single author;
- Duplication or the inclusion of material identical, or substantially similar, to material which has already been published, in another publication;
- Commissioning, stealing or acquiring material prepared by another person, and submitting it as your own work;

- Copying data/experimental results/statistics/references from whatever source (e.g. work of colleagues, notes provided on courses, textbooks, published reports) without acknowledgement;
- Copying tables, graphs, diagrams or other visual material without acknowledgement.

Quoting from someone else is acceptable so long as the source is acknowledged and cited (and so long as the amount of material contained within the quote is of a modest length). You cannot be accused of plagiarism if you have done this.

Good software systems exist today that exploit the power of free-text search to pick out similarities with other published material. Detecting plagiarism is easier now than ever before and is rapidly becoming easier still. To avoid all possible misunderstandings in anything you write, the message is: **Cite and reference all your sources**.

The nature of evidence

Evidence consists of the facts we extract from the sources of information turned up during our researches. We use these facts in statements that we assemble to provide what we hope is a logical argument leading to a satisfactory genealogical conclusion. That conclusion allows us to say 'this is who this person is' or 'this is how these people are related'.

In genealogical work, especially when identifying people in the past and linking them into family groupings to develop pedigrees, accurate information and incontrovertible facts are important. The picture we assemble that allows us to say who a person really is, and who they are related to, may come from a range of sources. Each source provides certain facts or assertions and these combine, we believe, to provide a coherent view that allows us to say with some degree of assurance that the person we are describing really is who we think.

The issue was described earlier as one of reliability, so let's digress for a moment into what that means.

If things are incontrovertible then they are highly reliable. However, we are often faced with information that is less certain and, therefore, less reliable. To build a case from this evidence we must be able to assess its reliability, and include that assessment in our arguments. We also must be able to place it in context with other evidence and show that there is no, or little, conflict between the various pieces of evidence that can be assembled. The accumulation of assessed evidence may reasonably substantiate our case.

The question then becomes, how do we carry out that assessment?

We have already dealt with the generally used distinction between primary and secondary sources. At first sight it seems as though primary sources must provide the better, more reliable facts. If only!

The first thing we must consider is that the records are all created by humans. The next thing to note is that humans are not very good at getting things right. We spell badly; we introduce assumptions whenever we think we know things already; we interpret in the light of what we have experienced previously, or what we believe. We live in a world where there is too much information gathered by our sensory systems. Our brain prevents overload by focusing on patterns recognisable from previous experience and it then predicts what should happen next. Indeed we 'see' what will happen next even when it does not happen – that is the basis for conjurors' success with close-up magic.

There is the famous example of 'Chinese whispers', where some phrase is whispered to the first person in a long chain then whispered in turn by each person to their neighbour. This results in a garbled message arriving at the far end, however careful each person believes they are being as they communicate. Transcription is an equivalent process in the world of records – errors will creep in. Assumptions are a key part of how we try to make sense of a complex world.

So how good is an old parish baptismal record? Well, it would not have been written by either of the parents. So, who provided the information and who wrote it down? Did the mother tell the cleric, or was it the father? Were the words mumbled, or in dialect? How long was it since the birth? How much did the excitement of the event affect memory? Was it two minutes before or two minutes after midnight? Did the cleric pass on the information to a recorder? Had the cleric scribbled a note to himself about it or was he relying on his memory – perhaps on a day when he had to deal with the affairs of two dozen other parishioners? Did the recorder write it down immediately? How sober was he?

Parish records occasionally go missing. In England, there is sometimes a substitute available in Bishop's Transcripts. These were copies that had to be sent in to the central administration of the diocese. Quite a relief to find them, but nevertheless, they are transcripts. By convention we treat the Bishop's Transcripts as primary sources (though we may fudge the matter by calling them derived primary). We must acknowledge that they are less reliable than the originals so we must also acknowledge that there is a spectrum of reliability.

Similar issues exist with census records. In UK censuses between 1841 and 1901 the householder was given a form to fill. Enumerators then copied the content into their schedule book and the householder's version was discarded. All that we know about today is the enumerator's version. It is the primary source, though it is 'derived'. Is it accurate? Well in the case of members of the Mewburn family of north-east England, about one third of them are enumerated as Newburn! If you were a Mearns living in Scotland you might naturally became McArns, as inbuilt assumptions about Scottish spelling kick in.

When assessing reliability of evidence and dealing with situations where the identification of individuals is rendered difficult through the presence of multiple candidates or conflicting evidence, we need to be explicit about the status of each piece of evidence.

In the USA, a quasi-legal approach is sometimes taken.[2] A proper distinction is made between types of source and the kinds of information they provide. Sources are described as original or derivative records, and authored narratives. Information is described as primary and secondary, or possibly even undetermined (where it is unclear whether it is based on first- or second-hand knowledge). The approach then goes on to categorise the evidence gleaned from the sources and the evidence they provide as being direct, indirect or negative.

If genealogical evidence is to be used in a court of law these distinctions may be helpful – though, as we have seen, it may be difficult to pin down the degree of originality of a record and the extent to which information is first hand. Arguably this approach adds precision. Alternatively, it can be thought of as over-analysed without adding the precision it imputes.

One thing we must be wary of when using any of these forms of classification or categorisation is the danger of ascribing significance to a thing because it has been given a classification. If something is declared to be original and primary that still provides no guarantee that its content is good. The content was created by people – and people make mistakes, it is the one thing you can be sure of. The categories are just labels. The assigned labels are only as good as the labeller.

All this categorisation can serve to provide a better understanding of the reliability of the evidence we are handling. It causes us to think about the material we have found. However, it is we humans who are doing the categorisation and we know how fallible we can be.

Our everyday use of primary source and secondary source conflates these ideas but remains adequate for most purposes. It helps us to think critically about the evidence we are using, and that is the key thing. Be prepared to question, and if necessary challenge, every piece of data you come across. Enjoy the process, though.

The other good news is that none of this categorisation business is incorporated into the way we write references.

Limits to evidence

As a final comment on evidence, and historical understanding, the novelist, Hilary Mantel, expressed the matter beautifully in her 2017 Reith lectures for the BBC:

> Evidence is always partial. Facts are not truth, though they are part of it – information is not knowledge. And history is not the past – it is the method we have evolved of organising our ignorance of the past. It's the record of what's left on the record. It's the plan of the positions taken, when we stop the dance to note them down. It's what's left in the sieve when the centuries have run through it – a few stones, scraps of writing, scraps of cloth. It is no more 'the past' than a birth certificate is a birth, or a script is a performance, or a map is a journey. It is the multiplication of the evidence of fallible and biased witnesses, combined with incomplete accounts of actions not fully understood by the people who performed them. It's no more than the best we can do, and often it falls short of that.[3]

Standards of acceptability in genealogy

Of course, citing the sources for all your evidence does not make your conclusions right. What is important is that the evidence should be used in a logical way to build a case from which conclusions can be drawn.

One approach is the use of the Genealogical Proof Standard,[4] a process developed by the Board for Certification of Genealogists in the USA (though not much seen outside their circle). It consists of the following:[5]

- Reasonably exhaustive research;
- Complete and accurate source citations;
- Critical tests of relevant evidence through processes of analysis and correlation;
- Resolution of conflicting evidence;
- Soundly reasoned, coherently written conclusion.

Sound enough advice, though the criteria for determining how you tell when any of these things has been satisfactorily achieved are unclear. The mix of both activities and outputs in the list is also a bit confused.

A very different approach comes from the discipline of nominal record linkage,[6] where a more mathematical model is used to determine how likely it is that named people are related. In essence, it follows a line of argument that says the greater the number of facts that match, the greater the likelihood of relatedness. The facts used are those gleaned from our cited sources.

The use of insights such as these should make it possible to assemble a set of statements of fact and supposition (premises) with, at the end, a conclusion. That is what a logician would call an argument. Genealogical acceptability is all about creating a successful argument from premises that can be seen to be true.

A difficulty in genealogy is that there is always an element of uncertainty. Truth turns out to be slippery.

The birth of a Joshua Meaborn to Jehoshaphat Meaborn and wife Belinda at Rye in March 1810 is likely to be unique, but it is not impossible that there was another Joshua born to different parents of the same names in the same place at the same time. The improbable does happen.

The further back we go, and the less informative the records become, then the more we are reliant on judgements about probability. Realistically, therefore, we need to revise our earlier statement to say that genealogical acceptability is all about creating a successful argument from premises that can be seen to be probably true.

You might, though, want to make use occasionally of the third Scottish court option. As well as guilty and not guilty, a jury in Scotland can opt for 'not proven'. That is often interpreted as 'we are sure you're a rogue but there is not quite enough evidence'. Something to consider when you are struggling with evidence.

The digital revolution

The nature of genealogical investigation has altered dramatically over the course of the past decade. The digitisation of documents and their availability online has transformed techniques of investigation and changed what we understand of the nature of sources.

The rate at which material is being digitised appears to be increasing exponentially and much of it is being made accessible online. Some archives have an explicit goal to digitise all their holdings and then to end access to original material except under exceptional circumstances. Stewardship of original material can then become a business process separate from the provision of information contained within the material. Security is tightened and costs lowered in consequence, while information access is simultaneously improved.

In this developing world, referencing then becomes a matter of pointing to the digitised images and their virtual location, perhaps in the Cloud, in contrast to that of a physical location denoted by a shelfmark. It does, however, raise questions over the stability or permanence of these virtual locations and over continuity and continuation of access. These issues will be dealt with later.

The materials we use and the places we find them

The digital revolution has not utterly changed our genealogical world. The materials we started out with are still there. They can still be found and examined, often very profitably. When we do find them, and take note of what they appear to be telling us, we can then let others know about our findings and where they can see things for themselves. The key to this sharing of information runs through the whole of our referencing. It comes down to being clear about what material we have used and where it can be found. This is equally true whether it can be touched and felt or just visualised in cyberspace. Whatever it is, wherever it is, we need to cite our finding of it.

The physical

Records are found on a variety of materials. Ancient writings appear on papyrus and bamboo. Vellum or parchment (prepared animal skin) is still used to inscribe the laws of England and carries many old court proceedings; more recently paper is the most common. Cuneiform writings on clay tablets appear in the Middle East from ancient times; nominal records can be found carved into and painted onto the walls of Egyptian monuments – so you can cite a tomb in the Valley of the Kings. Inscriptions in stone appear often; inscriptions on lead sheet appear in Roman times; names can be scratched onto glass; images of records are captured on microform rolls; digital images in the Cloud actually have a physical presence in mass storage associated with server farms in remote locations.

It matters little what the material is that has been used to carry a record when it comes to referencing it. Generally, when creating a reference, we do not make any mention of the material. However, it is occasionally something you may wish to take note of if there are issues of genealogical identification and the condition of the material, and therefore its accurate readability, becomes a matter for debate.

The places where we find our records are even more important, whether they be libraries, archives, burial grounds, war memorials or personal collections. A particular reason for citing sources is to direct readers to where they may see the same things that you saw. A precise address is essential (or perhaps GPS co-ordinates if you really are citing the Valley of the Kings).

The digital: written, spoken, video

Increasingly the materials held by libraries and archives are being digitised. Researchers are required to make use of the digital images and must reference them rather than the original material. It is the case already that in some archives the digital image is the only medium that can be consulted, except in exceptional circumstances. We must expect that this will soon become the norm in all major institutions.

The rate at which material is being digitised is increasing exponentially and it now includes spoken accounts of family history and videos capturing accounts of people and places of genealogical interest. YouTube has a growing collection of such things and it is reasonable that the genealogist should reference them.

Managed repositories of digital material are growing in line with the growth in what is available. Increasingly, that information will be made available only on a subscription basis as the repository managers engage archives in commercial partnerships.

At the same time, new free sources are appearing in the form of social media sites where information that could be referenced, mostly about the living, is available in astonishing quantities.

The researcher must now be prepared to explore all these avenues and identify the sources found.

Creating individual references: principles

In essence, what needs to be done is quite simple. You need to tell your readers who created the work you are referring to, when it was created, what it is called and who published it or where it can be found. You are providing co-ordinates that allow your readers to retrace your journey.

Who?
When?
What?
Where?

When we know 'who' we can make a judgement about the likely reliability of the creator; 'when' tells us either how close it is to acceptability as a primary source or whether it is from an era with different attitudes and mores; 'what' provides identity which may or may not be unambiguous; 'where' may also point to a need for examining social or political influences in our interpretation of the meaning of the material.

Most complications arise in determining who was responsible and where the thing can be found. That is particularly the case with digitised material made available on the World Wide Web – as we will see later.

Key elements and guidelines

Let's be more specific and start to consider the actual pieces of information needed in a reference and how we assemble them. In general, you should provide the following key elements (which you might imagine as fields in a database record or in a spreadsheet).

We'll start with secondary sources since these are the ones used most in scholarly writing, where the writers seek to dispute ideas among themselves. Genealogical work is different since it concerns itself more particularly with primary sources – 'hard' facts – but we'll come to that later.

These elements are typical of referencing for secondary sources:

- The author or organisation responsible for creating the work. [the latter is a 'corporate' author]. This is particularly relevant to secondary sources. With primary sources, as we will see later, if you are dealing with some kind of standard regulatory or administrative record this may be replaced by an indication of what type of generic record it is.

- The year it was published. [if there is one available]
- The title of the work.
- Where the work was published and who published it. [if a book or report]
- **Or** the journal where it appeared. [if an article]
- The page(s) cited. [of a book, report or journal article]
- The web address (i.e. URL) where it appeared. [if the text is located on the web]

You'll note that we put a full stop after each element to indicate its separate existence.

If you cannot find an example of the exact type of reference you need to create, then by including as many of the elements above as possible you should come up with an acceptable reference. You can always add a question mark within square brackets to indicate the information is not known [square brackets show that the information within is the voice of the person writing the reference; in other words … you].

The essence of referencing is that you provide enough information to enable others to track down, without too much difficulty, the source material that you have used.

The qualification 'without too much difficulty' is important, though. We do assume that those following the trail later are possessed of reasonable common sense and already have an appreciation of how archives work and of how the web needs to be approached.

Referencing is a skill that you will learn through practice; don't expect immediate ease with this process and in the words of a favourite guidebook, 'DON'T PANIC'.[7]

Characterising the source material

Every investigator needs to be very clear about the nature of each item of source material they use and about its reliability. Understanding the difference between primary and secondary information, and any derivation, and the sources that provide it is important.

This, however, is a matter for consideration during the analysis of that material, and for the building of logical arguments in support of genealogical conclusions. Classification of the nature of sources is not something that is included in a reference. The reference is there simply to enable that source to be tracked down.

Specifying the location

Location is important for at least two reasons. One is that knowledge of where an ancestor was at various times can help in assuring you that you really have got the right person. The other is that it enables those who follow your research to find the sources with as little difficulty as possible – avoiding the embarrassment of travelling to London, Ontario rather than London, England to find records.

The basic principle is to provide a reasonably full specification.

Places and county/shire names in references

Just a passing detail, but for the most part you should give place names as they appear in the source. That should always include the county/shire except when dealing with a few major capital cities such as London or New York. You should always include the country name too, as genealogy is rarely confined to a single country and because it avoids other forms of possible confusion, such as over London.

There are many examples of location references of different types later in this book.

Collections

When we think of 'where' any material can be found, the notion of a collection is useful. However, it appears in two different contexts. It is used in archives to refer to a body of material, possibly containing diverse kinds of things, that is kept together because it came from the same place or person, or some such reason. It is also used by us when dealing with online repositories to refer to a named database of closely related records, generally from the same point of origin. We will come back to these and use them to help pinpoint an origin.

Dealing with versions

Published material, most often from secondary sources, can be altered – sometimes quite often. Even primary sources can be subject to amendment or correction. When referencing a source, it is therefore essential to be quite explicit about the version you have seen and used.

Versions can be editions, reprints, prints in various countries, translations, hardback or paperback, e-versions and so on. The reference must be to the specific one you have used and it must state which one it was. For example, here are three versions of (almost) the same book:

Olle, T.W. et al. 1988. *Information Systems Methodologies: A Framework for Understanding.* Wokingham, England: Addison-Wesley Publishing Company.

Olle, T.W. et al. 1991. *Information Systems Methodologies: A Framework for Understanding.* 2nd ed. Wokingham, England: Addison-Wesley Publishing Company.

Olle, T.W. et al. 1990. *Méthodologies pour les systèmes d'information; Guide de référence et d'évaluation.* Paris: Dunod informatique. Translation in French of: Olle, T.W. et al. 1988. *Information Systems Methodologies: A Framework for Understanding.* 1st ed. Wokingham, England: Addison-Wesley Publishing Company.

In this case, if you were referring to the French edition it would be important to know that it is a translation of the first English edition.

Capturing the references

The basic principle is: do it as you go along. Write down the reference, in the full, correct format, when you first find information that you suspect you may wish to cite later.

If you are adding facts about a person in some genealogical software package then link them to the source reference as you do so. A package that does not allow you to do that should be avoided.

If you are writing things down as research notes then write the reference at the same time. If you are photographing material to study later then photograph all the title and publication details too. If you are recording someone talking about family matters then add your own voice commentary about time, place and participants. If you are working on the web then cut and paste URLs and DOIs (we'll talk about these later) into a notes system for easy future access.

To begin with it may seem irksome, but that is nowhere near as bad as trying to find the reference again from some scrappy note or half-remembered mental image of the glance at a document. Having to return to an archive at the other end of the country just because careful capture seemed too much trouble at the time is just the worst feeling.

4

The 'Harvard' style

The Harvard style or system of referencing is often mentioned. It is essentially a scheme for dealing with secondary sources. It has its origins in academic writing where the discussion and dissection of other people's ideas and writings plays a large part in the development of an argument on whatever the topic may be. The author is the key to citation in these disputations, so the author appears first in the reference. It is a wonderful approach but, as we will see, it is less well suited to the primary sources that play such a large part in genealogical investigations.

Origin; lack of a standard

Harvard University does not publish standards for referencing and never has.[8] The style is said to have been introduced, in his own writings, by Edward Mark, a professor of anatomy at Harvard in the nineteenth century. It then spread by word of mouth from others who read his work.

The referencing format we use for secondary sources and some primary sources is based on a modern re-interpretation of the Harvard style of referencing. There is no definitive Harvard style but it nevertheless exists as a strongly themed academic myth. It is a meme that went viral long before the viral idea was ever thought of. Strathclyde's Harvard format therefore may not match exactly those of other universities, but there are strong similarities.

Historically the Harvard style is an 'in–text' 'author–date' method, and would have been used by embedding citations in parentheses within the running text as in (Holton and Durie, 1884). That style serves when most citations are for secondary sources but does not work well for genealogical material where the great majority of sources are primary, lack an obvious author, and whose identification tends to require more elaborate means.

The style of citing and referencing that we do promote in this book (a not-really-Harvard style, if you like) is also called 'numeric' because superscript numbers are used to link the cited information to references held in separate notes areas. Numeric citation interferes less with readability than the author–date style. It also allows us to deal with the unusual sources favoured by genealogists, away from the main flow of our writing, by handling them in the notes sections where the references lie.

Publishers' tastes

What we suggest in this book will not be to everyone's taste. Individual publishers may insist on different formats for citation and referencing to conform with the particular typographical preferences their designers have determined upon.

If preparing material for publication, check with the publisher for details of their preferred style. References created using the guidance in this book will contain all the data needed. You should not need to do more than modify the format.

By far the most influential publication used by publishers, and one that will dictate many aspects of any written material, is *The Chicago Manual of Style*.

Chicago Editorial Staff. 2010. *The Chicago Manual of Style: The Essential Guide for Writers, Editors and Publishers*, 16th ed. Chicago: University of Chicago Press.

If you are writing material with a view to publication then following *The Chicago Manual of Style* along with this guide should stand you in good stead. Beware though that it offers advice primarily for conventional publishing practice, and not for genealogical practice with its focus on primary sources.

Some published versions

When it comes to Harvard style, currently the most influential guides are those published in the USA by the Modern Language Association and by the American Psychological Association.

Modern Language Association of America. 2016. *MLA Handbook*, 8th ed. New York: The Modern Language Association of America.

MLA is favoured by those aiming to publish academic material in the humanities and is widely used for teaching purposes. Its style is not dramatically different from that described in this book.

American Psychological Association. 2010. *Publication Manual of the American Psychological Association*, 6th ed. Washington, DC: American Psychological Association.

The APA manual goes into all the details of how to write and format written material, as well as dealing with referencing, so is in the same field as *The Chicago Manual of Style*. They claim social and behavioural sciences as their particular niche. APA use the embedded (author, date) method of citation that is not favoured here.

Unfortunately, neither the MLA nor the APA tackles the special needs of genealogy. This book rectifies that omission.

For a more UK-oriented view of the use of Harvard, there is a good overview of the style provided by the Anglia Ruskin University Library. You'll find that some of the elements are dealt with a little differently than our style but their examples are a good starting place for creating references for types of sources that are not tackled here. Naturally, you'll want to change their element layout to match ours.

> Anglia Ruskin University Library. *Harvard system of referencing guide*. http://libweb.anglia.ac.uk/referencing/harvard.htm.

The LearnHigher Centre for Excellence in Teaching and Learning has some great guides to why referencing is important, along with some online exercises and many examples of Harvard references.

> LearnHigher: Centre for Excellence in Teaching & Learning. *Referencing*. http://www.learnhigher.ac.uk/writing-for-university/referencing/.

An important source for genealogists is Elizabeth Shown Mills's *Evidence Explained*. It explores in detail the use of sources and the interpretation of their content. Its orientation is to the USA, and its approach is more prescriptive than European taste typically prefers. It eschews generic approaches and specifies a way of creating a reference for almost every imaginable source (though not some Scottish ones). That makes it difficult to use, as it runs to over 800 pages and some would describe it as an exercise in pedantry. However, though it may be overwhelming, it is a classic.[9]

> Shown Mills, Elizabeth. 2009. *Evidence Explained: Citing History Sources from Artifacts to Cyberspace*. 2nd ed., revised 2012. Baltimore, MD.: Genealogical Publishing Co. Inc.

We take the view that the use of generic categories, such as our 'source types', is a more manageable and usable approach to source referencing. Treating things in the same way that are broadly similar, and therefore share many characteristics, makes for an approach that is easier to learn and to apply. It has also allowed this book to remain short!

Using our 'Harvard' in the digital age

If you are creating a reference for an item that has been digitised and placed online, then approach the material like any physical book you might use and continue to include information on such details as the publisher's place and name. If the material is 'born digital', as some e-books or pamphlets are, there may not be a physical place of publication (or publisher's name) noted in the text so you won't be able to add that. If there is no date of publication, then give the probable year or range of year; (2010?) or (between 2000–2005). The crucial item for identification purposes will, of course, be the URL.

URL/web address guidelines

Subscription database URLs

There are several issues around the provision of URLs (Uniform Resource Locators or web page addresses) in references. These are to do with URLs for items found within subscription databases, the length of certain URLs and the use of 'root' URLs.

When you do a search within a database, the search engine creates a URL that gets displayed along with your search results. That URL describes the pathway followed to get to the information you asked for. That's the **whole** pathway. An equivalent in a library context would be something that says 'go in through the front door; take a slight left then go up the stairs to the first floor. On your left go through the double doors into Reading Room 1...' and so on. Very tedious, and quite unlike the practice of quoting a shelfmark. Humans can take certain things for granted and can be successful in finding material quickly when given a shelfmark. Computer systems usually take nothing for granted.

The resulting search-based URLs can be quite long and thus can use up large amounts of note space if used within a reference. A more important issue though is that these URLs are usually not 'fixed'. The website may be a dynamic structure subject to frequent change. Thus, if a user tries clicking on the cited URL, they may or may not be able to get back to the item you found earlier within the database, or to your list of search results.[10] Of course, if a user does not have a subscription when that is required for the database in question then any attempt to use the URL will fail. They won't be able to access the item without taking out a subscription.

Because of these issues, for references that deal with data found within most **subscription** databases, it makes more sense to give just the 'root' URL for that provider. This means giving the URL that takes the user to the home page of the website (akin, really, to identifying the publisher). The rest of the information given within the reference will enable future explorers to initiate a search to find the item again within that database, or indeed to find it among the original collection of documents.

'Short' or 'generic' URL provision covers such databases as: Ancestry; ScotlandsPeople; FindMyPast; most newspaper and article databases accessed through online providers, or a university website; Fold3; the Genealogist; MyHeritage; and others.

For example, here is a reference using a 'root' URL:

> Census returns. England. Bayton, Worcestershire. 31 Mar 1901. ACOCK, Thomas. ED 12; Piece 2515; Folio 142; p. 4. Collection: 1901 England Census. http://ancestry.co.uk.

Importantly there is sufficient information here to enable the original paper document to be tracked down even in the absence of the online source, so we do take a belt-and-braces approach to these references.

And here is the same reference using the entire URL copied and pasted from the web address bar at the top of the browser. You can see the difference in length!

> Census returns. England. Bayton, Worcestershire. 31 Mar 1901. ACOCK, Thomas. ED 12; Piece 2515; Folio 142; p. 4. Collection: 1901 England Census. http://search.ancestry.co.uk/iexec?htx=view&r=5538&dbid=7814&iid=WORRG13_2515_2517-0288&fn=Thomas&ln=Acock&st=r&ssrc=&pid=13496670.

'Regular' website URLs

The non-subscription database website, the Internet Archive, and 'regular' websites, give the entire URL of the web page you were using. Again, the URL can be found in the web browser address bar.

For example:

> Cracroft's Peerage. *Current Great Britain Baronetcies.* http://www. cracroftspeerage.co.uk/online/content/Curr%20GB%20Barts.htm.

Note that, unlike regular text, URLs are reluctant to allow a break in the string. This URL refuses to start on the first line and break in the middle. However, it is finally forced to break oddly at the end simply because the length of the indented line cannot accommodate it all.

There are further examples of references with URLs throughout this document.

'Fixed' database URLs

There are some databases that give 'fixed' or permanent URLs for search results – examples are: the subscription sites JSTOR and the *Oxford Dictionary of National Biography*, and the non-subscription FamilySearch. The URLs can be found in the web browser's address bar for these resources. For example, from FamilySearch:

> Baptisms index (PR). England. Whitby, Yorkshire. 05 Mar 1817. MEWBURN, Francis Clarke. Collection: England Births and Christenings, 1538–1975. https://familysearch.org/ark:/61903/1:1:J3FV-76B.

In this case the identifier at the end of the string – ark:/61903/1:1:J3FV-76B – provides the fixed link. If this URL is copied and pasted into the web address bar at the top of the page in your browser it should then open in the cited record.

Digital Object Identifiers

The Digital Object Identifier (DOI) is described as a 'persistent identifier' meaning that it provides a web address that is permanent. It can be thought of as akin to an ISBN number (the unique identifier you find in books) for digital material. These identifiers are now commonly found attached to published scholarly papers.

A DOI is assigned to a work at the time it is published. In appearance, the identifier is an alphanumeric string that begins with 10 and contains a prefix and a suffix separated by a slash. It is assigned by the publisher and maintained by a registration agency.

Where a DOI is available it should be included at the end of the reference. There are two acceptable ways of doing that – either as just the DOI or as a URL containing the DOI. For example, from the doi.org website:

- doi.org/10.1109/5.771073
- https://doi.org/10.1109/5.771073

The DOI, itself, will always lead to the right source so it is not necessary to include the full URL that may have led you to the item in the first place. If you try pasting the string from either of these examples, it will take you to the same place.

Permalinks

The permalink is another variation on the theme. It is particularly found in blogs where it typically acts as a permanent hyperlink to a web page or a blog post. Use these in the reference where appropriate.

6

Using 'Harvard' style for secondary sources

As we have stressed, there is no definitive 'Harvard' style. What is presented here builds on the ideas and structures discussed earlier. This chapter works through many, if not most, of the principal types of secondary source likely to be used by a genealogist. For each, it identifies the appropriate components of a reference and then provides examples to show how they would be applied in practice.

The punctuation in the bulleted guideline sections is the punctuation within the reference that is recommended when using that element. It is what *The Chicago Manual of Style* refers to as bibliographic punctuation. We use this to give a single format that is usable, without additional editing, for footnotes, endnotes and bibliographies. This is shown in the examples.

What follows is a number of sections each describing a commonly occurring kind of source. The elements used to compose a reference are identified and described. Examples of that kind of reference are given, along with brief comment on any notable features to help explain how variations can arise from the basic style the elements support.

Referencing a monograph

A monograph is perhaps the commonest type of secondary source you will refer to. It is simply a technical term for a publication devoted to a single subject. It may, for example, be a book, a pamphlet, a report or a guide. The term is, of course, an example of generalisation – the use of a single term to cover a range of superficially different things.

Elements in the reference are:

- Author(s) or editor(s). [with ed(s). if an editor or editors]
- Year of publication.
- *Title: subtitle*. [in *italics* and including the volume number if there is one]
- Edition. [if not the first]
- Place of publication: Publisher.
- Page number(s). [on which the data/quote appeared]
- Collection: Name of collection. [if the item was found within a database with multiple collections, then give the name of the collection]
- URL. [if the item was found online. See the URL guidelines for details.]

Notes on the elements

Author: The first element essentially identifies the originator of the piece or whoever it is who takes responsibility for it. It stands alone as a piece of information so we place a full stop after it.

Where the author is a person then the name is given as surname followed by given name. Some conventions have it the other way round. Our convention makes it easy to sort references into alphabetical order when creating a bibliography. We take it that consistency between referencing and bibliography is a sensible approach and that any approach that requires major re-formatting between one and the other is foolish.

We give the editor's name where the publication contains contributions from several people, and we place ed. or eds. after their name(s).

Where there has been joint authorship then in principle all authors are listed. However, this can become tedious when there is a long list so, by convention, when there are four or more we simply give the first author's name followed by 'et al.' – meaning 'and others'. This avoids a long-winded example such as:

> Olle, T. William, Jacques Hagelstein, Ian G. Macdonald, Collette Rolland, Henk G. Sol, Frans J.M. Van Assche and Alexander A. Verrijn-Stuart. 1991. *Information Systems Methodologies: A Framework for Understanding.* 2nd ed. Wokingham, England: Addison-Wesley Publishing Company.

Note that where we do specify multiple authors it is only the first one who has the name flipped and the surname given first (for easy sorting). The others are written with surname following given name (which conforms to *Chicago* style). This avoids messy and confusing placement of commas such as Olle, T. William, Hagelstein, Jacques, Macdonald, Ian etc. where we easily lose track of what are given and what are surnames.

The originator may be a defined responsible person, such as the head of a government agency required to present reports to parliament, even though that individual may not actually have written the report. Indeed, they may simply have commissioned it, but by doing so became the acknowledged originator.

The originator may be corporate rather than a person; in that case the name of the organisation is used. You can see that later in the Guild of One-Name Studies example. The National Archives in England is rather an odd case. It is commonly referred to with the inclusion of the definite article and abbreviated as TNA. Despite this, the definite article should not be used as the filing element in listings. The authority form for this corporate body, as established in the Name Authority File of the Library of Congress[11] is National Archives (Great Britain). This would be the best form to use when citing a work with this body as the corporate author – many countries have a national archive.

We've chosen to use this general authority form for other corporate body authors such as the War Office (Great Britain) and the Board of Trade (Great Britain).

A source without an author or editor's name will need to be shown in a bibliography using the title of the work. If the title begins with the word 'The', remove 'The' and list the source alphabetically by the second word in the title.

Occasionally you may come across something that has been translated or even transcribed. The good people who have done that work are not treated as originators, despite all their efforts. Instead, their names and role are given after the title of the work.

Other oddities crop up too. Occasionally, material that has not been published in a readily accessible form is re-published to make it more widely available. For example, Webster's census of Scotland for 1755 will be cited like this:

> Kyd, James Gray, ed. 1952. *Scottish Population Statistics including Webster's analysis of population 1755.* Reprint 1975. Edinburgh: Scottish Academic Press Ltd.

The bulk of the book's content is Webster's but he does not get to be named directly as the author of this publication.

An author's true identity may even be concealed. Anne Brontë's *The Tenant of Wildfell Hall* was published in the name of Acton Bell but, today, it would be pretentious to cite it as such since Anne is so well known in her real name.

On the other hand, the works of George Eliot and Lewis Carroll remain in those names despite having been penned by Mary Ann Evans and Charles Lutwidge Dodgson respectively. Accepted usage is the key.

A slightly trickier example is:

> Author of Johnny Gibb of Gushetneuk. 1877. *Notes and Sketches Illustrative of Northern Rural Life in the Eighteenth Century.* Edinburgh: David Douglas.

The actual author's name does not appear on or in this book (what is shown in the reference is what appears on the cover), and there is no modern re-published version that might give the secret away. However, the author is well known to be William Alexander, who produced a number of notable novels as part works in the *Aberdeen Free Press* newspaper (similar to the way his contemporary, Dickens, worked). Since we know him, it would be right to name him as the author, but in other cases this may not be possible so the reference in the form shown above might have to suffice.

Year: The second element is the year of publication given as a four-digit number with a full stop after it (older referencing schemes put the date in brackets but there is no compelling rationale for doing so, and in today's cleaner typographical approaches it is viewed as a visual distraction).

This information is not always readily available; if it cannot be found it must be omitted. This may be the case with ephemera such as published pamphlets. However, if there is a context that indicates the period when publication must have occurred it is acceptable to use the prefix *c.* (meaning '*circa*', or 'about') with a date – *c.* 1914. The document, even when undated, may itself contain information that dates it, for example the mention of dates for some events, so that the time range for its creation can be given, e.g. 1842–1846.

The lack of a date is common on material found in websites. It is important to check at the end of the item to see whether it is dated. It is also important to check the bottom of the web page where there may be a copyright date. The copyright date should be used in the absence of any date of origination.

Dates within a reference: When a full date appears, we use the genealogical convention and express it as dd Mon yyyy. Day is expressed as two digits, e.g. 09; Month is expressed as a three-letter abbreviation, e.g. Dec; and year is given in full as four digits, e.g. 2016. So: 06 Jun 1841.

Title: The title of a monograph is usually straightforward and is by convention italicised. Include the subtitle, if there is one, and do not introduce any punctuation (such as a comma or a colon) between the two unless that appears in the original. Sometimes there are variations between what appears on the cover and within the monograph. Use the version as it appears on the copyright page, if there is one, or on the half-title inside.

Note that we always say how many volumes there are if it is more than one. Note also that we do not italicise the statement of volumes.

Edition: When there have been multiple editions, the one used for referencing purposes must be identified. That is particularly important when also we cite page numbers as they may be unique to the edition. We use 'ed.' for edition and number it, so: 1st ed.

Publication: Place of publication and the name of the publisher are separated by a colon. This information is not always given on the monograph – so be it. Do not use the name of the printer instead.

Some Victorian antiquarian productions were published in several places and even by several different publishers. Include all the places and publishers (see the Worthy example).

If the place is a major city such as London or New York then that is sufficient on its own. Lesser-known places should be further qualified using a county or state name.

Page: As it says, the page number or numbers that are being cited. For a single page use p. and for several use pp. Always put the p(s) in lower case – it is just the convention. The page numbers are given at this point because everything that precedes them provides unique identification of the exact version of the publication you have been citing. It is *this* page in *this* document (whereas, of course, the information you want to refer to could be in a different place in any other version).

Incidentally, this book does not elide multiple page numbers. So, for example, it uses pp. 301–310, rather than pp. 301–10. That is just personal taste.

Collection: It is not unusual for records of a particular type, or on a particular subject, to be grouped together within a library or archive – 'British India records' or 'Business records' for example. If the material you are citing has come from such an archival collection then it should be named. We treat the various databases or record sets offered by online providers in the same way and give the name of the database or record set as a Collection name.

Online providers often acquire the rights to material from other repositories, such as The National Archives, but may have packaged it differently. A unique name may have been given to it and the span of time it covers may also be unique. For example:

Ancestry provides its:

England & Wales, Birth Index, 1916–2005
taken from material at the General Register Office in London.

FindMyPast offers:

England & Wales births 1837–2006 Transcription
also based on GRO material.

Each of these generic sources needs to be named as a Collection in your reference, and then followed by the URL for the particular provider. You will also need to consider the different ways in which this material has been treated when you evaluate the information they provide in determining the quality and reliability of the evidence that emerges.

URL: Finally, if you have acquired your information from online sources you need to provide the URL (unique resource locator), either full or generic, that will help the reader to get back to that particular source. More will be said about these later.

Increasingly there are permanent identifiers available for web-based material and these should be used where available.

Note that you will sometimes see references written with a date after the URL and a label along the lines of 'date accessed'. *The Chicago Manual of Style* is lukewarm on this convention.[12] They say it 'is of limited value' and 'Chicago does not therefore require access dates in its published citations of electronic sources unless no date of publication or revision can be determined from the source.'

The argument for putting it in is that material on the web often moves or is altered without warning, so putting a date acts as a claim by the citer that the information was accessible at that time. However, that is of no consolation to the reader who finds there is no longer a functioning link. Even when the link is still operative, the old date adds no value to the reference and does not help the reader to find the information cited. Don't do it, unless it is requested by a publisher or academic institution.

That being said, should you really want to trace the historic availability of something on the web, you may be able to find it using the Internet Archive's Wayback Machine, at archive.org. It provides access to hundreds of billions of archived web pages.

EXAMPLES

Tate, W.E. 1983. *The Parish Chest. A Study of the Records of Parochial Administration in England*. 3rd ed. Chichester: Phillimore & Co. Ltd. p. 58.

A basic example (for a genealogical classic), but showing that it is a third edition.

Wells, Harry Laurent. 1897. *Alaska and the Klondike: The New Gold Fields and How to Reach Them*. Portland, Oregon: [?]. p. 376. http://archive.org/details/cihm_16437.

Here the name of the publisher has not been discovered (of course, when faced with that, always check it out first through bibliographic sources such as www.worldcat.org). Should you read this book you may want to treat its advice with caution today.

Grant, James. 1880. *Cassell's Old and New Edinburgh: Its History, its People, and its Places*. Vol. 3. London, Paris & New York: Cassell, Petter, Galpin & Co. p. 8.

A multi-volume, multi-edition publication.

Worthy, Charles. 1898. *Devonshire Parishes: Or the Antiquities, Heraldry and Family History of Twenty-Eight Parishes in the Archdeaconry of Totnes*. Vol. 2. Exeter and London: William Pollard and Co. and George Redway. Collection: British Library 19th Century. http://www.jischistoricbooks.ac.uk/.

This has been published and does exist in a library collection but has then been digitised and made available for download from the web, which is where it was found. The URL is generic, however, and will not take you to the specific book; while the site itself requires an additional login from a subscribing organisation.

University of Strathclyde. 2017. *Genealogical, Palaeographic & Heraldic Studies*. Glasgow: University of Strathclyde. https://www.strath.ac.uk/courses/postgraduatetaught/genealogicalpalaeographicheraldicstudies/.

A straightforward example of publication on a website showing the path through the site. This, however, may change from year to year.

University of Dundee. 2017. *Postgraduate Courses in Family and Local History*. Dundee: University of Dundee. https://www.dundee.ac.uk/cais/programmes/familylocalhistory/postgraduatecoursesinfamilyandlocalhistory/#d.en.250123.

An example similar to the one before, and with the same caveat.

Herber, Mark. 2006. *Ancestral Trails: The Complete Guide to British Genealogy and Family History*. 2nd ed. Baltimore, MD: Genealogical Publishing Co. Inc.

Note that this is referencing an American printing of the second edition, though it was first produced in England in 2005. The version used must be the one cited. You cannot know what subtle differences may occur in a new printing. Note that this uses the standard two-letter abbreviation for the American state of Maryland. These abbreviations are quite acceptable for American sources.

Musgrave, Toby, Chris Gardner and Will Musgrave. 1999. *The Plant Hunters: Two Hundred Years of Adventure and Discovery Around the World*. London: Seven Dials. p. 76.

This has three authors so all are named.

Olle, T. William, et al. 1988. *Information Systems Methodologies: A Framework for Understanding*. Wokingham: Addison-Wesley Publishing Company.

This book has seven authors so we give just the name of the first one listed in the book's credits and use 'et al.' (*et alii* – meaning 'and others' in Latin) to indicate that there are several others (more than three is generally when we use et al.). Note too that this is the first edition but we do not say so since at the time of citation there may not have been a second one.

Guild of One-Name Studies. 2012. *"Seven Pillars of Wisdom" The Art of One-Name Studies*. London: The Guild of One-Name Studies.

This is the result of a team effort and there are no named authors. The organisation, therefore, is given the Author spot as well as being the Publisher. Note that we drop the definite article ('The') when making an organisation the author.

Durie, Bruce. 2009. *Scottish Genealogy*. Stroud, Gloucestershire: The History Press.

The county name has been included as part of the place of publication since Stroud is a small town not known to all. Using the name of a major city on its own is acceptable, but otherwise it is just polite to give readers sufficient information to avoid confusion. Note that you may want to advise people that the whole book is relevant so no page numbers are then included in the reference.

Mewborn, Michael Dennis. 2010. *The Descendants of Moses Mewboorn of England*. Lynchburg, Virginia, USA: Michael Dennis Mewborn. http://www.blurb.com/b/1479499-the-descendants-of-moses-mewboorn-of-england.

Here we have an example of self-publishing. The writer is both author and publisher, but production is carried out through a web publishing facility called Blurb. Incidentally, it is unlikely that the American Mewborns did come from England, but that's another story.

Bazewicz, Mieczysław, ed. 1991. *Architektura i technologia systemów informatycznych ISAT'91. Information Systems Architecture and technologies ISAT'91*. Wroclaw, Poland: Biblioteka Informatyki Szkół Wyższych.

Here the book carries titles in two languages (and contains papers in both languages, being conference proceedings). Both titles are given to ensure that it can be found in either language.

> Darwin, Charles. 1958. *The Origin of Species by Means of Natural Selection or The Preservation of Favoured Races in the Struggle for Life.* [*On the Origin of Species.* 1st ed. 1859. London: John Murray.] Mentor edition (paperback). New York: The New American Library of World Literature, Inc.

Great classic works, once out of copyright, can turn up in many forms. The one cited must be the one that appears in the reference. However, it is good practice to acknowledge how and when it started so the inquisitive reader can go back to a more 'original' source than this centenary edition. Note that Darwin saw it through six editions up to 1872. The notion of 'original' is not fixed, therefore – even as to the title. Which edition this inexpensive version is based on is not stated.

Referencing a monograph within a series

Organisations such as the Harleian Society and the Surtees Society have sponsored the production of numerous monographs. Each monograph is a separately published book but is also identifiable as a work within a series produced by the society. We treat these like books but also identify the series and volume number within the series, as appropriate.

Elements in the reference are:

- Author(s) or editor(s). [with ed(s). if an editor or editors]
- Year of publication.
- *Title: subtitle.* [in *italics* and including the volume number if there is one]
- Series title, and volume number.
- Place of publication: Publisher.
- Page number(s). [on which the data/quote appeared]
- URL. [if the item was found online. See the URL guidelines for details.]

EXAMPLES ───────────────────────────────

> Loyd, Lewis Christopher. 1975. *The Origins of Some Anglo-Norman Families.* Publications of the Harleian Society. Vol. 103. Baltimore, MD: Genealogical Publishing Co.

A fairly typical Harleian Society reference, though published in the USA.

> Littledale, A. Willoughby. 1895. *The Registers of Christ Church, Newgate, 1538 to 1754.* Publications of the Harleian Society. Registers, Vol. 21. London: Mitchell & Hughes.

In this case, there is a sub-series called Registers and the volume number is within that sub-series.

> Harleian Society. 1922. *The Visitation of the County of Rutland 1681–82.* Publications of the Harleian Society.Vol. 21. London: Harleian Society.

Often the Society is the only identified originator and can be its own publisher.

> Surtees Society. 1855. *Testamenta Eboracensia: a Selection of Wills from the Registry at York.* Part 2. Publications of the Surtees Society, Vol.30. Durham: Andrews & Co.

A typical Surtees Society reference. They are generally attributed as works by the Society and not to named authors.

Referencing a chapter in a book

Here we aim to deal just with a situation where chapters have different authors; in other words, where the publication is a compilation of some nature.

Elements in the reference are:

- Author(s).
- Year of publication.
- 'Title of chapter'. [within single quotation marks]
- In: Editor's name(s), ed(s).
- *Title of book.* [in *italics*]
- Place of publication: Publisher.
- Page number(s). [on which the data/quote appeared]

Notes on the elements

The rules are similar to those for a monograph except that we need the name of the chapter and its author as well as that of the book as a whole and of its editor – typically there will be an editor for this kind of book. In this situation, the book will not have a single author so we simply reference the author(s) for the chapter we are citing. The year of publication is for the book as a whole, but then we identify the title of the chapter we are focused on. It is placed within single quotes and is not italicised. That indicates its unique status as a chapter and later allows us to include the book title in italicised form as before. It means that our handling of the different kinds of information remains consistent.

After the chapter title, we reinforce its status as an independent portion of the book by adding 'In:' and also identifying the editor, before giving the full book title.

Publication and page details are then as we've discussed earlier. Note that we do not cite chapters in a book that has a single author – instead we would identify the relevant range of pages and include that within the reference.

EXAMPLES ──────────────────────────────

> Macdonald, Ian G. 1990. 'Automating information engineering'. In: Ince, Darrel and Derek Andrews, eds. *The Software Life Cycle*. London: Butterworth & Co. (Publishers) Ltd. pp. 329-343.

This is a standard example of this kind. Note the reversal of name format that is used when there are multiple named editors.

> Wrigley, E.A. and R.S. Schofield. 1973. 'Nominal Record Linkage by Computer and the Logic of Family Reconstitution'. In: Wrigley, E.A., ed. *Identifying People in the Past*. London: Edward Arnold (Publishers) Ltd. pp. 64–101.

This is again a standard example with the minor difference that Wrigley is both editor of the compilation and a contributor to it, so he appears in both contexts. Note the reversal of name format that we use when there are multiple named authors.

> Burns, Rev. James. 1833. 'Brechin, County of Forfar'. In: *The Statistical Account of Scotland 1834–45*. Vol. 11. pp. 134-141. http://stat-acc-scot.edina.ac.uk/link/1834-45/Forfar/Brechin/.

This is a very different example where the publication is an official government report. However, it is a compilation of entries, effectively chapters, each for a parish and each written by an incumbent cleric at that parish. Generally speaking, each writer dates their own piece which is how in this case it is earlier than for the overall publication which does not have a single year of publication.

> Shrimpton, Jayne. 2011. 'Dating Family Photographs: Researching Victorian and Edwardian Photographers and Studios'. In: Blatchford, Robert and Elizabeth Blatchford, eds. *The Family and Local History Handbook*, Vol. 13. York: Robert Blatchford Publishing Ltd. pp. 22–28.

This is from an unusual publication that combines magazine and directory elements in a more-or-less-annual book. Treating the articles in it as book chapters works well enough, and treating the whole thing as a book rather than a journal or magazine means that more publication details can be given.

Referencing a dictionary or encyclopaedia entry

Dictionaries and encyclopaedias are assemblages of entries, and you may or may not know who was responsible for each of them. They are, in principle, quite similar to the book with different authors for different chapters.

Elements in the reference are:

- Author(s) or publisher name. [publisher given if there is no author name]
- Year of publication.
- 'Title of entry'. [within single quotation marks]
- In: *Title of dictionary or encyclopaedia.* [in *italics*]
- Place of publication: Publisher.
- Page number(s). [on which the entry occured, if using a print version]
- URL. [if the item was found online. See the URL guidelines for details.]

EXAMPLES ──

Bell, William. 1861. 'Jus Mariti.' In: *A Dictionary and Digest of the Law of Scotland.* Edinburgh: Bell and Bradfute. p. 497. http://archive.org/details/adictionaryandd01rossgoog.

In this example, Bell is the author responsible for the whole book and all the entries. In principle, therefore, you could just cite the whole book and a page number. However, the form of referencing shown above allows attention to be drawn to the single topic that is the focus for discussion.

Hey, David, ed. 2010. 'ceorl'. In: *The Oxford Companion to Family and Local History.* 2nd ed. Paperback version. Oxford: Oxford University Press. p. 312.

We do not know who wrote this entry as authorship is not credited for items in the A–Z section of the book. David Hey is therefore named as the editor. We have also specified the book format since, though the content may be identical between hardback and paperback, pagination may differ.

Hey, David. 2010. 'The Poor'. In: *The Oxford Companion to Family and Local History.* 2nd ed. Paperback version. Oxford: Oxford University Press. pp. 206–213.

Here, Hey is credited with having written this section of the book so appears as its author.

Oxford University Press. 1976. 'liquor.' In: *The Concise Oxford Dictionary of Current English.* 6th ed. Oxford: Oxford University Press. p. 633.

Here the individual entries do not have named authors and neither does the book, so a corporate originator is named for the book.

Referencing a biographical or alumnus entry

People of a certain standing in society do like to see their names in print, and this can be invaluable to the genealogist. A range of publications exist that catalogue members of the nobility and gentry and provide a certain amount of biographical detail. Others list notable people of the time or of a particular profession. In some respects, they resemble the directories that are discussed later, or the dictionary entries discussed above.

Many educational institutions also publish histories with details of past pupils. These too are secondary, being compilations created after the event – quite different to school yearbooks that are contemporary and can be rated as primary sources.

Elements in the reference are:

- Author(s) or publisher name. [publisher if there is no author name]
- Year of publication.
- 'Title of entry'. [within single quotation marks]
- In: *Title of biographical listings*. [publication name in *italics*]
- Place of publication: Publisher.
- Page number(s). [on which the data/quote appeared, if using a print version]
- URL. [if the item was found online. See the URL guidelines for details.]

EXAMPLES

Burke, Sir Bernard. 1906. 'Mewburn.' In: *A Genealogical and Heraldic History of the Landed Gentry of Great Britain*. 11th ed. London: Harrison & Sons. pp. 1154–1155.

The Burke family, over several generations, created a publishing empire based on a range of titles and many editions. Care should be taken over which Burke is the author. The common usage of 'Burke's' for them all is not good enough for a reference.

Pirie-Gordon, H. 1937. 'Mewburn (now Mewburn-Watson) of Acomb.' In: *Burke's Genealogical and Heraldic History of the Landed Gentry*. 15th ed., part 2, London: Shaw Publishing Co. Ltd. p. 1585.

Note. The author of a Burke's may not be a Burke.

Peerage. 2015. 'Sir Alexander Gibson, Lord Durie.' In: Lundy, Darryl, compiler. *The Peerage*. http://www.thepeerage.com/p41947.htm#i419469.

This is purely a website and as Lundy styles himself 'compiler' that is respected in the reference so he does not appear in the author slot. In this case, the year of publication is the date of last update to the cited entry.

Black, A. & C., eds. 1961. 'Mewburn, Sydney Chilton.' In: *Who Was Who, 1951–1960*. London: Adam & Charles Black Ltd. p. 760.

Who's Who and *Who Was Who* are both excellent sources for the more notable members of society.

Hall, Douglas. 2006. 'Douthwaite, Patricia Morgan Graham (1934–2002).' In: *Oxford Dictionary of National Biography*. Oxford: Oxford University Press. http://www.oxforddnb.com/view/article/77051.

Here, each entry is separately authored so Hall is responsible for the named entry. The ODNB is one of the great sources for the UK genealogist, at least when again chasing more notable members of society. However, a subscription is required to gain access – but many libraries will have one.

Mennell, Philip. 1892. 'Mewburn, William Richmond.' In: *The Dictionary of Australasian Biography*. London: Hutchinson & Co., Supplement. p. 536.

Many countries have their own biographical publications.

Society for Recognition of Famous People. 2016. 'Anderson, Elizabeth Garrett.' *The Famous People*, website. www.thefamouspeople.com/profiles/elizabeth-garrett-anderson-6282.php.

An example of a wholly online resource. This begs the question, can you be famous and unrecognised?

Caniff, William. 1894. 'Dr. Francis Clarke Mewburn.' In: *The Medical Profession in Upper Canada, 1783-1850: an historical narrative, with original documents relating to the profession, including some brief biographies*. Toronto: William Briggs. p. 514.

Histories of a profession often carry biographies of noted practitioners.

Royal College of Physicians. 2009. 'Hugh MacLean'. In: *Munk's Roll, Lives of the Fellows*. Vol. V. p. 257. http://munksroll.rcplondon.ac.uk/Biography/Details/2882.

A typical entry from this online resource.

Cambridge University Press. 1922–1954. 'Mewburn, James. 1782.' In: Venn, J.A., compiler. *Alumni Cantabrigiensis: a biographical list of all known students, graduates and holders of office at the University of Cambridge from the earliest times to 1900. Part 1, From the earliest times to 1751*. London: Cambridge University Press. Collection: Cambridge University Alumni, 1261–1900. www.ancestry.com.

The University Press is given as the originator since Venn is billed as the compiler rather than author. Entries in this carry a condensed summary of lifetime events. It could be consulted in either physical printed form or online – in this case online.

Foster, Joseph. 1888–1892. 'Butler, William Somerset, 1735.' In: *Alumni Oxoniensis: The Members of the University of Oxford, 1715–1886*. Oxford. Parker & Co. www.ancestry.com.

And a similar example for Oxford. Foster's role may have been similar to that of Venn at Cambridge, but he is not billed as a compiler, so is given author status.

Referencing a journal paper or magazine article

Academic journals may be printed in many volumes over many years but by convention the complete set is treated as a single publication. Editors are generally not acknowledged. References focus, therefore, on individual papers and their author(s), and on when they were published.

Magazine articles can be treated similarly as may items in other forms of periodical. Newspapers are dealt with later.

Elements in the reference are:

- Author(s).
- Year of publication. [if available]
- Title of article. [without quotation marks or italicisation]
- *Title of journal*. [in *italics* because this is the name of the publication]
- Volume number(part number), Month. [by antique convention no space is allowed between the volume and part numbers. The month is included if available. Magazines may not appear with volumes and parts and may be identified just by date]
- Page number(s). [on which the data/quote appeared]
- Collection: Name of collection. [if the item was found within a database with multiple collections, then give the name of the collection]
- URL. [if the item was found online. See the URL guidelines for details]
- DOI. [a Digital Object Identifier if the paper has been published in an online journal that subscribes to such a service]

Notes on the elements

If you are citing material (e.g. a journal paper) found in an online database, reference it as you would any other journal paper and add the root URL or the fixed URL for the database in which it was found, or the DOI for the paper itself. If the paper was found within a subscription database, you may need to give the name of the collection in which the paper appeared, if it cannot otherwise be easily found.

EXAMPLES ————————————————————————

Geuss, Raymond. 2002. Genealogy as critique. *European Journal of Philosophy*. 10(2). p. 210. http://onlinelibrary.wiley.com/.

Available online, through a subscription website, so a URL is given, but note there is no month of issue. This paper deals with genealogy as a philosophical construct and not as most readers of this book may think of it.

Beer, M. and N. Nohria. 2000. Cracking the code of change. *Harvard Business Review*. May-June. pp. 133-141.

The standard form of a journal paper, but with the publication quarter and no volume or part.

Maddicott, J.R. 2011. The Oath of Marlborough, 1209: Fear, Government and Popular Allegiance in the Reign of King John. *English Historical Review*. 126(519), April. p. 283. http://www.jstor.org/stable/41238641.

A full reference for a printed journal which is also available online and was consulted in that form. Note that it has a fixed URL.

[No author]. 1861. The Genealogy of Christ. *Journal of Sacred Literature and Biblical Record*, Apr. 1855–Jan. 1867. 13(26), April. p. 335. Collection: British Periodicals. http://search.proquest.com/.

Material consulted from the online repository of a subscription site. The citer has commented that the identity of the author has not been found.

Plant, Dr. John S. and Prof. Richard E. Plant. 2015. Surname Simulations, DNA, and Large-Descent Families. *Journal of One-Name Studies*. 12(3). pp. 18–20.

Family history journals carry a wealth of valuable material including novel research techniques. In this case identification follows the issue(part) style of scholarly journals.

Harper, Marjory. 2012. Adventures of a 20th-Century Fur Trader. *Aberdeen & North-East Scotland Family History Society Journal*. 123, May. pp. 44–47.

Articles are commonly specifically family history and genealogical in nature. Here the identification is not by part within issue; each publication has a unique serial number with the month of publication.

Thomas, Jenny. 2011. Using Historical Newspapers. *Who Do You Think You Are?* 48, June. pp. 16–21.

Family history magazines may also carry material that is worth citing. Note that the issue month is being used as a qualifier to help identify it.

Macdonald, Ian G. 2017. Mewburn: London Silversmiths. *The Journal of Genealogy and Family History.* 1(1). pp. 1–12. https://doi.org/10.24240/2399 2964.2017.030101.

A conventional reference, but one that provides a DOI. The publication is a rare example of a scholarly journal outside the USA in the field of genealogy.

Knauft, Bruce M. 2017. What is Genealogy? An Anthropological/Philosophical Reconsideration. *Genealogy.* 1(1), 4. doi:10.3390/genealogy1010005.

This is an online publication with papers numbered in each part and with no page numbers in the streamed version. A PDF download does have page numbers so care must be taken to use that version when citing a quotation. It also shows the DOI in a different style. This paper deals with genealogy as a philosophical usage in the Nietzschean and Foucauldian tradition – possibly an acquired taste for readers of this book.

Referencing a conference paper

Although the items in the proceedings from a conference may look like journal articles, this kind of publication is a one-off production. The proceedings typically appear after the conference and will, almost certainly, have an identified editor. The treatment is therefore more like that of a book with separately authored chapters.

Elements in the reference are:

- Author(s).
- Year of publication.
- 'Title of paper'. [within single quotation marks]
- In: Editor(s) names, ed(s). *Title of conference proceedings.* [in *italics*]
- Name, place and date of conference.
- Place of publication: Publisher.
- Page number(s). [on which the data/quote appeared]

EXAMPLES

Urtin, David J. 2000. 'The information professions in the new century'. In: Hapling, Alan, ed. *The new information professionals.* Proceedings of the European Conference of Librarians and Information Scientists, Brussels, 4–6 September 1998. Aldershot, UK: Gower. p. 65.

A typical example of a conference paper reference.

Macdonald, I.G. and R.A. Veryard. 1995. 'Modelling business relationships in a non-centralized systems environment'. In: Sölvberg, Arne, John Krogstie, and Anne Helga Seltveit, eds. *Information Systems Development for Decentralized*

Organizations. Proceedings of the IFIP working conference on information systems development for decentralized organizations. Trondheim, 1995. London: Chapman & Hall. pp. 133–167.

Evidently the references can be fairly lengthy in the case of more academic conferences but the detail needs to be provided nonetheless.

Harper, Marjory. 1995. 'Bridging the Atlantic: Mechanisms of Scottish Emigration in the 19th Century.' In: *Hands Across the Water: Emigration from Northern Scotland to North America.* Proceedings of the 6th Annual Conference of the Scottish Association of Family History Societies. Aberdeen, 22 April 1995. Aberdeen: Aberdeen and North East Scotland Family History Society. pp. 1–17.

Another example of these unfortunately long-winded references. In this case, no editor is acknowledged in the publication.

Referencing an unpublished thesis or dissertation

A great deal of valuable research work is undertaken by students, particularly when working towards higher degrees such as Masters (MSc and MLitt) and Doctorates (PhD and DPhil). The end product may be called a thesis or a dissertation. There is no significant difference between these terms. Only a few are published in an accessible form. Traditionally they have ended up on shelves in the university library, though the advent of digital technology has altered that. If they can be found they can be read – often quite profitably – so they need to be cited.

Elements in the reference are:

- Author.
- Year of creation.
- *Title of dissertation.* [in *italics*]
- Type of dissertation. [generally qualified by Unpublished]
- Place: Awarding institution.
- Page number(s). [on which the data/quote appeared]
- URL. [if available in digitised form for downloading]

EXAMPLES ──

Brown, Stephen. 1994. *The impact of information technology on management functions and structures.* Unpublished MSc dissertation. Glasgow: University of Strathclyde. p. 26.

Note that here we are citing some comment made on a particular page.

Increasingly, dissertations are being digitised and made available online. In these cases, it may be the version found online and downloaded that needs to be cited. Here are relevant examples that can be found within the British Library EThOS service.

Fenwick, Carolyn Christine. 1983. *The English poll taxes of 1377, 1379 and 1381: a critical examination of the returns.* Unpublished PhD thesis. London: London School of Economics and Political Science. www.uk.bl.ethos.263359.

The whole work is being cited as something that is very useful when genealogy gets back to the fourteenth century. This is a wonderful source.

Durie, Bruce. 2011. *Bringing History to the Public via Genealogy and Family History.* Unpublished PhD thesis. Glasgow: University of Strathclyde. www.uk.bl. ethos.618852.

Again, a reference covering the whole work since it carries interesting observations on the state of genealogical practice.

Referencing an archived letter

Material that has ended up in an archive may not have been published but can be accessed by those following your path in research. In this case, the letters are unlikely to be to you and are more likely to be between people you are researching and mentioning in your text. In these cases, the reference is fairly straightforward and can include a pointer to where the item is held and where others can find it.

There is a catch here, however. These letters may be part of a dialogue with a correspondent – providing thoughts, comment and opinion on matters of interest to the author. Such letters are secondary sources, like other things in this chapter. However, other letters can deal with immediate matters, and recount details of events the author has recently been involved with. They are primary sources.

Your reference will not distinguish between secondary and primary. It is up to you to make that distinction within your text and point out the significance to your readers.

Personal correspondence is often primary, and is dealt with in chapter 12.

Elements in the reference are:

- Author.
- Date of correspondence.
- Type of correspondence. [letter – and description used by the archive]
- Archival collection name. [if applicable. This only needs to be given if found at an archive where the material is placed in a named collection]
- Archival reference. [the code used to identify the item in the archival system]
- Repository location: Repository name. [the place and name for the archive]

- Collection: Name of collection. [if the item has been digitised and was found within a database with multiple collections, then give the name of the collection]
- URL. [if the item was found online. See the URL guidelines for details]

EXAMPLES

Anderson, John [1726–1796, natural philosopher]. 13 Feb 1750. Letter from John ANDERSON at Glasgow to Mr. Gilbert LANG at Lossitt, to the care of Mrs. LANG at Greenock. Collection: John Anderson Papers: General correspondence. Ref: GB 249 OA/2/1. Glasgow, Scotland: University of Strathclyde Archives.

This appears within a body of material relating to Anderson so is identified as within that archival collection. It is also identified through an archival reference code which indicates where it is now physically stored.

In this case, a note has been inserted in square brackets to show that the author was a distinguished person. Generally speaking, this should be unnecessary within a reference as it should have been made clear in the text at the point of citation. Note, too, that surnames are in capitals to show they are of genealogical interest.

Mewburn, James. 1798. Letter to William Pitt jun. Piece ref. PRO 30/8/158. Kew, London: The National Archives.

This archived letter is treated like any other material from an archive, unlike personal correspondence you may need to cite. This is material that is available for public access at the archive.

7

Cloud sourcing

Digital material provides a new set of challenges for source referencing. Some of the technical matters have already been discussed; some examples of source referencing are offered here.

E-mails and web pages have a clear line of descent from letters and books but new challenges arise when we must deal with e-books and even more so with forms of social media. Whether the latter are even fit to be cited may be argued.

Referencing an item of personal e-mail

This is today's equivalent to citing a letter received. E-mails are sometimes thought of as ephemeral though, in practice, they may be held on local servers or in Cloud storage for many years (as malefactors in various fields are finding). It should be possible to be very precise in citing this kind of communication.

Elements in the reference are:

- Author.
- Year of correspondence.
- *Subject line.* [in italics]
- Type of correspondence, day and month, time.
- Recipient's e-mail address. [if a personal e-mail address, request permission before publication of document]

EXAMPLE

Wakeford, R. 2002. *Standards of service in the library*. E-mail to William McGonagle, 12 July, 15:06. mcg@dis.strath.ac.uk.

Only include the actual e-mail address with the permission of its owner.

Le Grande, Monique. 2013. *Re: Question regarding Beatrice Le Grand's birthplace*. E-mail to Jean Boulique, 13 July, 12:14.

Note the precise time, to the minute, in both examples.

Referencing an item read on an electronic mail discussion list or forum

The informal nature of some electronic resources can pose problems if you want to cite them in references, as the information you require may not be immediately obvious.
Elements in the reference are:

- Author.
- Year.
- *Subject line.* [title of discussion; day and month and time of post if available]
- Forum or discussion group. [its name – akin to a publisher, though with no place of publication]
- URL. [see the URL guidelines for details]

EXAMPLE ───

Durie, Bruce. 2015. *Online one year full-time MSc genealogical, palaeographic and heraldic studies at the University of Strathclyde, Glasgow.* Register of Qualified Genealogists, LinkedIn group. https://www.linkedin.com/.

This comes from a discussion group hosted on LinkedIn. Membership of the group is needed before access to anything posted there is permitted so only a generic URL is used. The full URL would fail to link without appropriate access permissions.

Bannister, Carol. 2017. *Using English Ecclesiastical Court Records for your Family History.* Video, 17 Sep. Register of Qualified Genealogists, Facebook page. https://www.facebook.com/RegQualGenes.

All sorts of material can be posted on Facebook. This is an example of a short video, highly informative, appearing on a public Facebook page established by a non-profit organisation dedicated to the improvement of genealogical practice.

Referencing an item from an online blog or vlog

Blogs provide news (and gossip) and opinion items offered up online by the creator of the blog or vlog. Responses and comments by readers can also be captured.
Much of what appears is recycled material, not original, but there may be occasions when something deserves to be cited. Video material often takes the form of short training courses.
Elements in the reference are:

- Author(s). [blog/vlog creator]
- Year of publication. [if available]
- Title of post. [without quotation marks or italicisation]

- *Title of blog or vlog.* [in *italics* because this is the name of the publication]
- Date of posting. [day and month – and time, if recorded]
- URL. [See the URL guidelines for details]

EXAMPLE ————————————————————————————

Eastman, Dick. 2017. Oklahoma Birth and Death Record Indexes are now Online. *Eastman's Online Genealogy Newsletter.* 10 Jan 2017. https://blog. eogn.com/2017/01/10/oklahoma-birth-and-death-record-indexes-are-now-online/#more-16712.

This blog is treated as a publication akin to a magazine, and the item is treated like a magazine article. This particular blog is one of the most notable in the field of genealogy.

If you want to cite a comment appended to a blog posting then treat it as something within that posting:

Colby, Guy I. VI. Comment. 11 Jan 2017, 09:44. In: Eastman, Dick. 2017. Oklahoma Birth and Death Record Indexes are now Online. *Eastman's Online Genealogy Newsletter.* 10 Jan 2017. https://blog.eogn.com/2017/01/10/oklahoma-birth-and-death-record-indexes-are-now-online/#more-16712.

This is listed just as a comment as it has no title of its own. The full date and time of posting is included since that provides an accurate audit trail through other comments.

Referencing a web page

Websites and pages on them vary considerably when it comes to providing any means of identifying when, and by whom, the content was created and made available. This is particularly true when the website is corporate in nature. Content may have been created by a web designer or by a marketing department without any expectation that it might be used in a reference, or at least that any individual should be credited.

Elements in the reference are:

- Author(s). [this will often be a 'corporate' author]
- (Name of place of publication and/or name of web page publisher). [if identification would otherwise be unclear]
- *Title of web page.* [in *italics*; if the author and title of the web page is the same, just give the author's name]
- URL. [see the URL guidelines for details]

Notes on the elements

As we all know, addresses (URLs) for web pages can fail so if you give just a URL as a point of reference when referencing a web page, your reader may not be able to find the source again. This is why it is essential to provide additional identification details for web pages because if you can search for a page's title or author, you may be able to find the page again at its new location.

Providing these additional identifiers for web pages is often tricky as it can be difficult to determine what the title is, or who the author is. Looking for an 'about us' section can help to find an author's name and often you'll need to make an educated guess as to the title of the web page.

Just remember that the main point of providing references is to enable your reader to find the information again, so if you have used an internal page within a larger web page, then consider giving the title of that internal web page as well as the name of the larger website. Or if it's unclear which of many potential entities a web page refers to, give the name of the place of origin or name of the web page publisher within square brackets. Sometimes a copyright claim at the bottom of a web page can be helpful as a way of indicating who is taking ownership.

If the author and title of the web page are one and the same, just give the information once.

You may be creating a reference for a book, pamphlet or other item originally published in physical format that has been digitised and made available online through providers such as the Internet Archive, Google Books, or others. In that case, approach the reference like any physical book and include information on publisher, place and name. The same goes for digitised articles that were originally published in physical format that you've found online in databases such as JSTOR (a system for providing online access to scholarly content for the academic community). See the monograph and article sections for more details on referencing these.

EXAMPLES

Farrell, Stephen. *Hanoverians: Parliament and Politics from George I to the Reform Act of 1832.* http://www.historyofparliamentonline.org/periods/hanoverians.

In this case, the author is named so the reference can be attributed to him.

National Library of Scotland. Website. http://www.nls.uk/.

Here the institution is credited as the author and since the title of the web page is the same it is not repeated. This reference is just to the NLS website as a whole, and leads to the home page.

National Library of Scotland. *Map images.* http://maps.nls.uk/.

Here the web page has a subtitle, so that is included and the URL is now more specific.

National Archives and Records Administration (United States). *Research our records.* https://www.archives.gov/research.

Compare with:

> National Archives (Great Britain). Website. http://www.nationalarchives.gov.uk.

In these two cases, it could be unclear which of the many national archives around the world were being referred to, so the countries are named as well as giving the generic URL from the website.

> University of Portsmouth, et al. *A vision of Britain through time: Census Reports.* http://www.visionofbritain.org.uk/census/.

The website is produced through a collaboration among several institutions with Portsmouth appearing first.

Referencing information found using an e-book reader

A variety of devices exist that allow e-books to be read, for example Kindle, Kobo, Nook and iPad. If you have downloaded a book to play on such a device then it is reasonable to cite that book. However, each kind of device may handle the digitised material in its own particular way, and differences in format may result.

On the whole, the approach to e-referencing is still to follow the general referencing style for monographs (or journals, etc. depending on the item). However, there are a few minor changes that need to be made depending on the formatting of the e-book reader or e-book file used. Add the word 'version' following the type of e-book (e.g., Adobe Digital Editions version, Kindle iPad version, Nook eReader version).

A significant issue arises where the software dynamically adjusts the display to match the size and resolution of the reading device. This means that pagination is different to that of a print version of the material. In some cases, no page numbers are displayed, in others the page numbers do not remain constant when you enlarge the text or switch between different display devices.

The structure of the text will not change, however. Parts, chapters, sections and so on remain as created by the author. This is true right down to the paragraphs used and the sentences they contain.

The safest form of reference is therefore based on the author's structure so you can locate the information you want to cite by detailing something such as – chapter 4; section 2 (if there are subdivisions within the chapter); paragraph 5. This provides close equivalence to citing a page number.

Going so far as to number specific sentences is unnecessary, and citing a paragraph is also unnecessary when a whole section is the subject of the reference.

Conventional referencing may still be possible. For example, some Kindle books will include page numbers that match print. They are displayed next to locations when you push the Menu button.

Remember, the main aim of references is to allow your reader to return to the information you used, so for resources whose 'shape' varies from user to user you need to focus the reference on those features that do not change.

Elements in the reference are:

- Author(s).
- Year.
- *Title*. [in *italics*]
- Edition. [if more than one]
- [e-book type].
- Place of publication [if available]: Publisher.
- e-book source URL.
- (Part number [if there is one], Chapter number: heading(s), Section: title [if there is one], Paragraph number). [on which the data/quote appeared]

EXAMPLES

Denscombe, Martin. 2014. *The good research guide: for small-scale social research projects*. 5th ed. [Kindle version] Maidenhead: Open University Press. http://www.amazon.co.uk. (Part 1, chapter 1: surveys, section: response rates).

This example uses the author's structure to point to the area of interest.

Oates, Jonathan. 2012. *Tracing your ancestors from 1066 to 1837: a guide for family historians*. [Kindle version] Barnsley: Pen and Sword. http://www.amazon.co.uk. (Chapter 1: The state and church, 1066-1837, section: Tudor and Stuart England, 1485–1714).

Another example similar to the previous one.

8

Referencing for genealogical and archival sources

Some theoretical background

In principle, genealogical records are ones that provide data we might wish to use to create a database to hold all the information that goes into building a family tree. It makes sense, therefore, to structure references to these records in a way that is in line with the kind of structuring we might employ when designing such a database.

There are well understood principles for doing this, based on the idea conjured up in the 1970s of 'normalisation'[13] where each type of record describes just one thing and one thing only, and contains attributes specific to just that one thing. It is easy to say but harder to get your head around.

Figure 1 illustrates a portion of the kind of data model that might be used to describe such a database.[14]

Paper records can carry data about a diverse range of things. Database technicians will describe these 'things' as 'entity types' or 'objects'. So, Person would be an object of interest, as would Country, and these are quite different concepts. We could think of Birth, Death and so on as types of object or we might be more generic and use a term such as Life Event to cover all births, baptisms, deaths and burials. The detail is

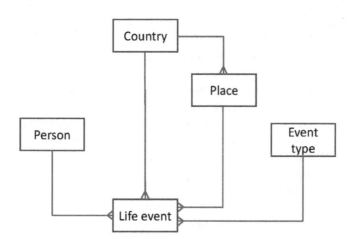

Figure 1. Some genealogical data.

not important. We just need to recognise that paper records generally contain a mish-mash of bits of information describing a bunch of different things needed for various administrative purposes (not all of which have genealogical significance). In principle, it is good practice to keep these things separate in our reference and we do that simply by putting a full stop after bits of information that belong to different objects.

We will also want to be clear about the various *types* of source records that are being used to provide the data we need. It helps to have a way of classifying these sources so that we can establish a common way of handling each.

Genealogical sources and their classification

Versions of the Harvard referencing system do include ways to deal with many primary sources; some examples include maps, letters, newspaper articles, interviews, websites and Acts of Parliament. However, they are rarely as good when it comes to many of the types of records that genealogists work with day in and day out. Many of these are primary sources and have been created through some form of administrative process. They are records to capture 'facts' rather than opinion (as is the case in secondary sources) so we are not concerned with knowing the identity of an author whose views we may wish to place under scrutiny. By contrast, we are concerned with the kinds of records that can provide information of genealogical relevance, and with understanding just how relevant they might be.

As a result, we've created guidelines on how to deal with the principal types of sources you will be working with. There is a vast array of sources so it is convenient to group them in ways that help us understand what areas of commonality they share. Things can make a bit more sense when they are grouped, or classified.

The challenge is a little like the one that faced the great Swedish biologist, Linnaeus, when he was establishing his scheme for classifying organisms in the natural world. He placed closely related species together in a 'genus', where there is a sharing of certain 'generic' characteristics. Genuses (*genera* if you prefer to remain faithful to the Latin), he then grouped into 'families' – where there is a 'family' resemblance.

For example, to the genealogist all birth records are trying to do a similar job. However, at different times and under different administrations, the way they do it may not be quite the same in detail. Nevertheless, 'Births' can be used to describe a group of closely related records that make up a type of source. For the most part, we know what to expect from something called a birth record. If you like, 'Births' is akin to the genus. Our equivalent to the species might then be 'Births in an old parish record from Wales'. That is a bit cumbersome, so we will use a simpler scheme for naming such things.

The following guidelines and examples cover *some* of the main types of sources likely to be referenced. If there is not an example for the type of resource you are using, then by following the 'non-standard' general principles below should allow you and your reader to find the resource again.

Major source categories

As a researcher, you are faced with a multitude of different kinds of records. The number and range of these is increasing as our society seeks to administer and measure more aspects of existence. That provides more opportunities for research but can add confusion when trying to determine what value new sources may add to an investigation. It may also make the task of referencing seem more daunting.

It helps to consider what the records are primarily about. We can think of them falling into three categories of record:

- Nominal;
- Material;
- Procedural.

If you want to go back to Linnaeus, then these are akin to 'families', but we are starting to beat the analogy to death, so it won't go any further.

Note, there is nothing formal, fixed or canonical about these categories. They are being used simply as a convenient way to divide things up and to help understanding. If you are searching for sources, you might also want to explore records that exist because of an individual's chosen engagement with social matters or those that have been imposed on the individual to serve society's administrative purposes. The three categories used here simply represent one point each of perspective.

Nominal records are essentially to do with people. They name the people they relate to – hence nominal. These are the records that genealogists devote most of their time to, and include births, marriages, deaths, census returns and various lists and directories.

Material records are to do with things. They record information about these things, and among that information may appear the names of people who are in some way associated with the things. These things may be buildings, parcels of land, cars, works of art, shareholdings and so on. They may provide valuable information about the people associated with them, and that may in turn help to flesh out aspects of the peoples' lives and histories.

Procedural records are to do with procedures – events or activities or systems set up by us to help the smooth running of our society and businesses. Again, people get caught up with these and may be named. These happenings include court cases, accounts of football matches, records of purchases made from a company, payroll records that list the people receiving payment, and a multitude of other involvements. They, too, are valuable for family history purposes.

In practice the ways in which we reference things from among these source categories do not differ greatly, but it will be helpful to illustrate their treatment individually and show examples from each category.

It is also worth saying that these categories are being used in this book primarily to help us organise our thoughts about the various kinds of things that turn up. Records from the nominal category are the ones that genealogists generally start with, rely on most, and mine for detail most assiduously. However, that does not make them 'better' than others and the mere fact of having suggested three categories does not mean that any one is more reliable than any other. Each type of record, from whatever category, needs still to be assessed on its own merits.

Source types

Similar kinds of record are found in different administrations around the world and in a range of separate archives and repositories. It is madness to define a particular way to reference each and every one of them. Instead we take a generic approach and classify the commonest of them (and therefore the ones we will use most often) within what we call a *source type*.

Source types for the nominal category are particularly helpful since they provide a consistent means of handling the data elements from records that direct us to individual people. These types cover the vital records of birth/baptism, marriage/ partnership and death/burial and include most of the other significant kinds of life events that we use to further characterise the main features of an ancestor's existence.

Source type list

For UK vital records we qualify the source type by acronyms descriptive of the period and origin of those records. These acronyms are:

- OPR = Old parish records [Scotland];
- PR = Parish records [England/Wales/Ireland];
- NCR = Non-conformist records;
- CR = Civil records.

The standard source types using these acronyms then become:

- Births (OPR) / Births (PR) / Births (NCR) / Births (CR);
- Baptisms (OPR) / Baptisms (PR) / Baptisms (NCR);
- Banns (OPR) / Banns (PR) / Banns (NCR);
- Marriages (OPR) / Marriages (PR) / Marriages (NCR) / Marriages (CR);
- Deaths (OPR) / Deaths (PR) / Deaths (NCR) / Deaths (CR);
- Burials (OPR) / Burials (PR) / Burials (NCR).

Note that the name for a source type is always given in the plural – Births or Deaths – because the type refers to all those records in the category.

Note also that many of these source types and their qualifiers can be used perfectly well for countries other than the UK. Baptisms (PR), Births (CR) and so on are terms that can be applied in Australia, Canada, the USA and elsewhere – wherever you find church records or civil records. For example, in the nineteenth century, Jewish births in Kraków were required to be recorded by the Roman Catholic Church, so they can be referenced as 'Births (PR). Austria [Poland].' – bearing in mind that Poland did not exist as an independent state at that time.

Our other standard source types for frequently occurring records that are nominal, in that they are essentially about identifying people in various contexts, are:

- Births (RCE) / Marriages (RCE) / Deaths (RCE) [a unique bunch – RCE = Scottish Register of Corrected Entry records];
- Birth announcements / Marriage announcements / Death announcements [typically from newspapers];
- Census returns;
- Electoral listings;
- Directory entries;
- Membership listings;
- Service records;
- Obituaries;
- Testamentary records;
- Monumental inscriptions;
- Grants of arms.

It is worth adding that these source types are recommendations. They are not carved in stone.

If you need to reference a type of source that is not covered in this list, for example a letter found at an archive or some farm accounts, then use the format described later for a non-standard record.

Again, most of these source types apply just as well to equivalent records found in countries other than the UK so we use them in those contexts exactly as we do for the UK records.

In one particular respect, some of these source types are specifically UK oriented. That shows up in the use of (PR) and (NCR) as qualifiers for some church records. These come about through the idea of the 'established' church in the UK. (PR), when used with English records, means that they are from the Church of England, while with Scottish records it means they are from the Church of Scotland. (NCR) means they are from any other church – Roman Catholic, Episcopalian, Methodist, Unitarian, Hindu, etc. However, when dealing with records from other countries (PR) will point to records from the predominant church in that country, for example in Italy or Poland it will mean Roman Catholic.

We always give the country name after the source type to ease this interpretation, but an alternative would be to add the church type after (PR) as in (PR, Church of England) or (PR, Free Church of Scotland), and not use (NCR). It is more elaborate but also more explicit. Examples in this book do not go that far.

Note, too, that the actual records are not necessarily all clean primary sources. Monumental inscriptions may not be contemporaneous and the identity of those who commissioned them is often uncertain; newspapers often repeat information from unknown sources; census returns are often transcriptions by an enumerator made on an unknown date, and so on.

Sources for sources

A vast array of sources exists, particularly when you consider the many countries through which you may want to trace people. This book touches on and provides examples of many sources but comes nowhere close to all those available or those that might become available through the exponential growth of the digitised world.

For those who might want to explore less-trodden paths it is worth consulting:

- *Ancestral Trails* by Mark Herber.
- *Sources for Local Historians* by Paul Carter and Kate Thompson.
- *Understanding Documents for Genealogy & Local History* by Bruce Durie.
- *Tracing your Irish Ancestors* by John Grenham.
- *The Source* by Loretto Dennis Szucs and Sandra Hargreaves Luebking.

This is a small selection (referenced fully in the Bibliography), but they cover a lot of ground. Bear in mind that source types are used only for the most commonly occurring or used kinds of sources so generic referencing will be the answer for many of the rarer documents mentioned in these books.

Records and indexes

Over the years, armies of volunteers and, more recently, paid helpers have worked to make genealogical information more accessible to researchers by creating indexes to original source records. These indexes will generally show that there exists in some record source, from a given place, a record for a named individual for an event in their life on a particular date. The index entry may contain additional facts from the record, but index entries do not purport to be transcriptions of the whole record (even when sometimes they declare themselves to be a 'transcription').

In a perfect world, the genealogical researcher would always work from original primary records, or good images of them. Cost is, however, a barrier. If records have not been digitised it is often the case that they can be obtained solely from governmental sources and only in the form of 'authorised' copies. These are usually expensive.

The practical effect of this is that research often depends on significant use of indexes, with full record copies being obtained only where the resolution of identities is proving difficult. However, uncertainty is introduced by reliance on indexes and it is essential that the researcher makes clear in a reference whenever a source is an index rather than the full record.

The additional qualifier 'index' is used with the source type when the record accessed is not either an image of the original or a complete transcription of the original, e.g. Births index (CR) or Burials index (PR). FamilySearch records, for example, though they may show most of the information in a record do not display it all, and are described by FamilySearch themselves as indexes. Many record sets provided by FindMyPast are described as transcriptions but are not complete, so are better referenced as indexes. Increasingly, though, images of the original record are provided along with the index entries. The researcher should always go to the image, and reference that, rather than rely on what has been transcribed.

Belt and braces

Another simple principle that should be followed in structuring a reference to a genealogical source found online, is to give the reader the security of having two ways to find it: the belt-and-braces approach. We do that by including information that identifies where the original record can be found, as well as where it has been found in online form. The reader can then search for it either in an archive or online, as the mood takes them.

We do this only when the record has been found online, rather than examined in its original form, perhaps displaying a bit of paranoia towards our technology and ignoring humanity's capacity for destroying the past. Rapid obsolescence in all forms of information technology makes this a wise precaution, however.

General structure for genealogical references

In essence, the bits of information making up a genealogical reference fall in two parts – one that characterises the kind of information the reference deals with, the other providing clues to where the source can be found. The first part consists of:

- Source type;
- Country;
- Place;
- Date;
- Person.

These cover the nature of the information and the context for it – the What and the Who.

- Archival reference;
- Collection;
- URL.

These do the belt-and-braces thing, where the archival reference points to the original document, while collection and URL point to where it may be found online – the Where.

So, the first part tells your reader what there is to find while the second part says where to find it.

More formally, the components use the following format:

- Source type. [see above for a list of source types]
- Country.
- Place. [format is: smaller area first followed by larger area, then any identifier numbers that relate to those areas]
- Date of event. [registration/entry/etc. (dd Mon yyyy: 12 Aug 1946 or 03 Jul 1645)]
- Name(s). [using the genealogical format: SURNAME, First (and Middle) name. This is the person to whom the record refers for citation purposes, or both people in the case of a marriage/partnership]
- Archival reference. [The style may vary from country to country, for example]
    - ScotlandsPeople data number. [only for Scottish records. This unique reference number is given for many records found on ScotlandsPeople. It is the same as the former 'GROS code']
    - Volume or register number.
    - Page number, entry number.
- Collection: Name of collection. [if the item was found within a database with multiple collections, then give the name of the collection]
- URL. [if the item was found online. See the URL guidelines for details]

Note that the records used in different places, and at different times, can vary greatly in format and content. They were not designed for genealogists to use! It may not be possible, therefore, to include all this information. A record simply may not include it. Correspondingly, in some other situation, you might identify other pieces of information that would be more applicable.

The punctuation in these bulleted guideline sections is the punctuation within the reference that is to be used for that element. Please refer to the examples as well for guidance on using punctuation within references.

If a source is a transcript of a record and is thus not an actual record (i.e. the image of a census page or birth certificate), then that must be acknowledged in the reference. That may be by describing the source as an index, or by saying that the collection consists of transcripts.

If a source has been accessed online, this *must* be acknowledged by giving the web address, the URL, of the source.

As always, the key principle is to provide information enough to let other people get back to where you found the information you have used.

9

Nominal records

This is the first of our three major source categories. It contains records that are to do with people, and that name those people. These are the lifeblood of genealogy and where genealogical investigations typically start.

Referencing BMD records

These are what we often call 'vital records'. They are those that record the key milestones in a life – birth, marriage and death. However, it is often not quite like that. Church records (the bulk of older records) view this from the perspective of church membership so use baptism and burial as their start and end points.

Civil records, focused on births and deaths, are there for governments to know when they can tax people, and when their responsibilities to provide support, begin and end. Church records are there to lay claim to the person in some spiritual sense within its ministry.

BMD records are some of the most important to any genealogical investigation. Elements in the reference are:

- Source type. [as listed earlier, e.g., Births index (CR); Baptisms (OPR) [Scotland], (PR) [England/Wales], (NCR) [Non-conformist Register], Marriages (CR)]
- Country. [this always qualifies the source type as specific formats of record vary from place to place]
- Place. [e.g. Townland / Parish / County / State, or any other place name that would be helpful for identifying the record]
- Date of event, registration quarter or entry. [For quarter, use either number or bounds of quarter e.g. Q1 or Jan – Mar]
- NAME(s), given name(s). [for the person being born/baptised, persons being married/named in banns; person dying/being buried]
- ScotlandsPeople data number. [Scottish records only. Other providers may also offer unique identifiers, e.g. Durham Records Online have an individual Record Number, so that should be included here]
- Registration District; Volume or register number.
- Page number.; entry number.
- Collection: Name of collection. [if the item was found within a database with multiple collections, then give the name of the collection.

You do not need to do this for ScotlandsPeople since it is the only online source for original source images]

- URL. [if the item was found online. See the URL guidelines for details]

Note that it may not be possible to include all this information and you might identify other pieces of information that would be more applicable in a particular case.

Note, too, that in published governmental indexes for civil registrations the district given will be the registration district. That may be different to the more specific location name the people would typically use to describe where they live.

Where they are available, it is good practice always to capture both birth and baptism details and reference them seperately. Baptismal records, on their own, can be misleading since the ceremony can take place long after the birth – sometimes years later. The place where a baptism takes place may also provide a poor clue as to where the family was living.

Banns, too, are records that need to be treated with care. They may be read in more than one parish, often in parishes where the bride or groom originally came from. Banns are also not a substitute for a marriage record – the marriage did not always follow and, sometimes, the marriage could take place some considerable time after the banns.

You are mostly on safer ground with burials. They typically took place soon after death. However, the place of burial may be distant from the place of death, especially where there is a family link or a family burial plot. However, you won't often come across cases where the dead person is not actually buried, as with the philosopher Jeremy Bentham, whose preserved remains are on display at University College London.

EXAMPLES: BIRTHS AND BAPTISMS

Births (CR). Scotland. Kelvin, Glasgow. 10 Jul 1910. MCCALDEN, Archibald Weir. 644/13 0778. http://www.scotlandspeople.gov.uk.

Here 644/13 0778 is the ScotlandsPeople GROS data number, a unique identifier that includes the registration district number (644), the register number (13) and the registration district entry number (0778) specific to that particular record. GROS is a hang-over from the days of the General Register Office for Scotland but the number itself continues to be used by National Records of Scotland.

Births (CR). England. St. Heller, London Borough of Sutton. 05 Feb 1972. BEECHING, Gerald. Entry no. 151.

This example results from obtaining an actual copy of an entry in the register of births for the Sutton registration district; there was no register number apparent on the copy. An original document is referred to, hence no URL is involved.

Births index (CR). England. Blackpool and Fylde, Lancashire. Jan 1995. MATTHEWS, Mary. Register C40C. Entry no.155.

As this index is post-1984, the year and month of registration is available instead of just the year and quarter.

> Baptisms (NCR). England. Haverhill, Suffolk. 08 Nov 1818. WEBB, Martha. RG4/1794. Collection: Non-Conformist and Non-Parochial BMDs. https://www.thegenealogist.co.uk.

An English non-conformist example, available online. The title of the collection from the online provider is given, as is the code used for archiving at The National Archives where the originals are held.

> Baptisms (NCR). Scotland. Montrose Street Congregational Church, Glasgow. 16 Jul 1898. (Birth: 10 Jul 1898). WILSON, John. GB 243 TD1332. Glasgow, Scotland: Glasgow City Archives.

In this case GB 243 TD1332 are the repository and reference codes for this non-conformist baptismal register held at the Glasgow City Archives. The register was viewed in person and not many of the 'normal' pieces of data we add to references were available. By including the collection codes and the name and place of the archive, your reader knows where to access the register.

It so happens that in this register entry the date of birth was also given. It is not required for the reference but you can show such information in round brackets if you feel it would be helpful to the reader.

> Baptisms (OPR). Scotland. Gorbals, Lanarkshire. 29 Aug 1835. CAMPBELL, David. 644/02.

The example is for a record viewed on microfilm. The code 644/02 is the parish number/volume number In this case Gorbals had not yet become a part of Glasgow, thus the addition of the county name is necessary and was shown on the record itself.

> Baptisms (OPR). Scotland. Chapel of Garioch, Aberdeenshire. 18 Jun 1826. ALEXANDER, William. 179/ 20 43. www.scotlandspeople.gov.uk.

The example is for a record image viewed on ScotlandsPeople. The code 179/ 20 is the parish number and volume number, and 43 is the page number. William Alexander became editor of the *Aberdeen Free Press* and a noted author in the Doric dialect of the northeast.

> Baptisms index (PR). England. Swaffam Prior, Cambridgeshire. 26 Oct 1628. LARKIN, Alice. Source film no: 1040550. Collection: England Births and Christenings, 1538–1975. https://familysearch.org/ark:/61903/1:1:NKK8-B79.

This is taken from FamilySearch and here it helps with identification to add the name of the internal database, which in this case is 'England, Births and Christenings, 1538–1975'. We add it as a Collection. The URL is a fixed type. FamilySearch properly describe their records as Indexes; though they are transcribed they are not full transcriptions, so we use Baptisms index as our source type.

> Baptisms index (PR). England. Swaffam Prior, Cambridgeshire. 1628. LARKIN, Alice. Collection: England Births & Baptisms 1538–1975 Transcription. www.findmypast.com.

This is the same record as the one above, but taken from FindMyPast where they describe the internal database as a Record Set, in this case named 'England, Births & Baptisms, 1538–1975 Transcription'. We add it as a Collection. Note that though the record is described as a transcription it is not a full transcription (and does not have the full date of baptism) so we use Baptisms index as our source type (in fact the origin of this data is acknowledged as FamilySearch index records – see the previous example).

> Baptisms (PR). England. Egglescliffe, County Durham. 23 Oct 1698. MEEBURN, Abigail. Rec. No: 1165297.0. Collection: Baptisms, Stockton District [transcription]. http://www.durhamrecordsonline.com/.

This subscription database has many collections covering all record types and has a unique identifier for each record. It does not display a URL that shows the full search path so only the generic URL is appropriate. They do provide a full transcription of the original so these references are not treated as 'index' records; however, to make the position clear, it is helpful to the reader to add the comment [transcription] in square brackets after the collection name. Note that this differs from the situation above where FindMyPast uses 'Transcription' as part of its collection name, yet does not provide a complete transcription.

> Baptisms index (PR). England. Ormesby, Yorkshire. 27 Sep 1759. MEWBURN, George. Film no: 919075. Collection: England Births and Christenings, 1538–1975. https://familysearch.org/ark:/61903/1:1:J3XQ-Z4Z.

The online record for this reads:

> Name: George Mewburn
> Gender: Male
> Christening Date: 27 Sep 1759
> Christening Date (Original): 27 Sep 1759
> Christening Place: Ormesby, York, England
> Father's Name: George

Compare this with another transcription of the same parish record that goes:

1759
Mewburn, George; f George, butcher; Sep 27

That small difference, the word 'butcher', makes it possible to correctly assign the birth father, as there was another George, a farmer, in the area at the same time.

A reference for the latter transcription is:

Baptisms (PR). England. Ormesby, Yorkshire. 27 Sep 1759. MEWBURN, George. In: Breckon, C., transcriber. 1992. *Ormesby Registers: Christenings 1703–1899*. p. 11. Shelfmark YK/REG/73285. London: Society of Genealogists Library.

We might expect this source to provide a full transcription but given the difference between the two 'transcribed' sources the researcher should at this point consult the original record or the film of it.

EXAMPLES: BANNS AND MARRIAGES

Banns (PR). England. Grosmont, Yorkshire. 26 Nov 1899. SHAW, George Henry and MORGAN, Jane Anne. Page 77, No. 226. Collection: Yorkshire Banns Image. www.findmypast.com.

The last of the banns dates has been used to identify this source. Note that records of banns are often annotated with the date of the marriage and, when they are, they can reasonably be cited as a record of marriage. In this case, the marriage date is not given.

Marriages index (PR). England. Hastings, Sussex. 02 Jan 1840. ROSE, Philip and RANKING, Margaretta. Source film no: 1067178. Collection: England Marriages, 1538–1973. https://familysearch.org/ark:/61903/1:1:NK4F-5MG.

A conventional reference for a FamilySearch index record, including the fixed URL. Note that we include the names of both parties to the marriage.

Marriages (PR). Wales. Worthenbury, Flint. 24 Feb 1719. NEWENS, John and MORGAN, Elizabeth. Collection: Diocese of Chester Bishop's Transcripts of Marriages c.1600–1910 Image. www.findmypast.co.uk.

FindMyPast provides a 'transcript' of this record and a scanned image of the original. Where this is the case the original should always be consulted and cited in preference to the 'transcript'. In this case, the information that John is 'of the parish of Whitchurch in the County of Salop' is said, in the transcript, to be his birth place though it may just be his residence, while the 'Bride's residence' section of the transcription is left blank though the record seen in the image describes her as 'of this parish'.

Because this is a Bishop's Transcript in the first instance you, as a researcher, have to be doubly cautious in your interpretation of how good the information is.

> Marriages (CR). Scotland. St.Andrew, Edinburgh. 07 May 1891. WHITE, Andrew and KING, Elizabeth. 685/02 205. http://www.scotlandspeople.gov.uk.

This is a standard civil record reference for a marriage in Scotland.

> Marriages (RCE). Scotland. Milton, Glasgow. 26 Jul 1870. ARBUCKLE, Andrew and DARROCH, Margaret. 644/07 002 0132. http://www. scotlandspeople.gov.uk.

This provides details of a correction to the original marriage record (denoting a divorce). The date in this example is, therefore, that of the RCE (Register of Corrected Entries) entry, not the marriage itself. The ScotlandsPeople data number is also different to that of the actual marriage. The RCE reference is found on the original marriage record of 06 Dec 1864.

> Marriages (PR). England. Durham Diocese, County Durham. 11 Jul 1798. JOHNSON, Thomas and MEABOURN, Ann. Record Number: 455668.14. Collection: Marriage Bonds, Durham Diocese District [transcription]. http://www.durhamrecordsonline.com/.

Marriage Bonds appear when a licence to marry is issued rather than banns being read. The Bond is an indicator of a marriage rather than solid evidence of it having taken place. Records are sometimes annotated with the actual date of marriage.

> Marriages (PR). Scotland. Gretna Green, Dumfriesshire. 10 Jul 1803. MEWBURN, Tulip [July] and ARMSTRONG, Betty. Collection: Marriage Registers, Gretna Green, Scotland, 1794–1895. www.ancestry.com.

An example of a Gretna Green marriage. Scotland has always been quite accepting of irregular marriages. Proclaiming your state to be married in front of witnesses sufficed. Since lengthy residence was not required either, and Gretna Green was close to the border with England, it became, and remains, a popular place to do the deed. Note that the wrongly transcribed given name of the groom is added in square brackets to assist researchers.

> Marriages (PR). England. Fleet Prison, London. 27 Aug 1740. HARRISON, Samuel and ASHBY, Mary. Collection: Non-Conformist and Non-Parochial BMDs. www.thegenealogist.co.uk.

Marriages at the Fleet (a debtors' prison) are often called clandestine, though they did involve a clergyman. After the Marriage Duty Act of 1695, banns or a licence were required for a marriage. The prison and its environs lay outwith church control so those rules did not apply and faster, cheaper marriages could take place, without questions asked. In the early eighteenth century about 12 per cent of all the marriages in England took place there. Hardwick's Marriage Act of 1753 ended this practice (but there was still Gretna Green).

EXAMPLES: DEATHS AND BURIALS

Church records generally provide details of burials, while the state concerns itself with deaths – with varying rules for when such information can be released online. Increasingly, details of modern-day burials can be found in announcements on undertaker's websites. These are contemporaneous and can be treated as primary records even without a government seal of approval – though with the usual caveats about accuracy from, in effect, a third party.

Here are some examples:

> Deaths index (CR). England. Houghton, Durham. Jul–Sep 1873. CHURCHILL, Frances Ann. Vol. 10a. p. 305. http://www2.freebmd.org.uk/.

In this case, the county name of Durham is not displayed in the search results and it is necessary to follow a link from Houghton to get that information.

> Deaths (CR). Scotland. Aberdeen Northern District, Aberdeen. 05 Jun 1945. MACDONALD, George Riddel. 168/1 633. www.scotlandspeople.gov.uk.

A standard Scottish death reference where the image of the death record has been viewed.

> Burials (PR). England. Whorlton, Yorkshire. 07 Nov 1746. HUGIL, Miriam. Collection: Yorkshire Burials Image. www.findmypast.com.

A standard reference where an image of the parish register is available online (and additionally gives the husband's name). There is also a transcript, but that should not be referred to when the image is available.

> Burials (OPR). Scotland. Edinburgh, Midlothian. 02 Dec 1727. ANDERSON, James. 685/1 880/334. www.scotlandspeople.gov.uk.

A typical Church of Scotland old parish burial record.

> Burials (NCR). England. Bunhill Fields, London. 02 Feb 1830. MEWBURN, John. RG4. Piece 3998. Collection: Non-Conformist and Non-Parochial BMDs. www.thegenealogist.co.uk.

RG4 is the identifier for The National Archives' collection 'Non-parochial Registers 1567–1858'. Bunhill Fields is a noted non-conformist burial ground (now a public garden in Islington maintained by the City of London).

> Burials index (PR). England. Manfield, Yorkshire. 19 Apr 1803. WITHAM, Catherine. In: *National Burial Index*, 3rd ed. 2010. Manchester: Federation of Family History Societies & Associates.

The National Burial Index is a magnificent source. It is, though, still a long way short of providing comprehensive cover for parish records and it provides only a basic content rather than a complete transcription.

> Burials (NCR). Scotland. Muchalls, Kincardineshire. 21 Jan 1820. SPARK, John. In: *St Ternan's Episcopal Church Muchalls. Register of Baptisms, Burials and Marriages*. Muchalls: St Ternan's Episcopal Church. 2003.

This is a Scottish non-conformist record and comes from the digitised Register (on CD) created by Dundee University Archives department and indexed and published by members of the congregation.

> Burials (CR). England. Eston Urban District Council, Yorkshire. 28 Feb 1945. MEABURN, Matthew William. No. 6056. Collection: Deceased Online. www.deceasedonline.com.

UK burials are not subject to centralised registration, as are deaths. However, this record on a subscription site has been gathered from a local authority, so is still viewed as a civil record.

EXAMPLES: OTHER JURISDICTIONS

In **Australia**, online indexes are provided separately by each state government. Some records can also be found through online database providers.

> Marriages (CR). Australia. Launceston, Tasmania. 26 Aug 1846. ACKLIM, Henry and WATTS, Mary. RGD37/1/5 no 144. Rec. Id. 834115. http://www.linc.tas.gov.au/family-history/Pages/Birth-Death-Marriage.aspx.

Tasmania provides images online for many records, unlike most states at this point, so we are not dealing with an index record in this instance. The URL is to the introductory page from which a name search leads to the record.

> Deaths index (CR). Australia. Chiltern, Victoria. 1888. CANNY, Mary. Reg. No. 12811. https://online.justice.vic.gov.au/bdm/indexsearch.doj.

An example from Victoria where the Justice Department provides a website but with indexes only. Some records may give places of birth and death and the name of a spouse.

> Deaths index (CR). Australia. Victoria. 1877. DUNCAN, Jane. Reg. No. 11281. Collection: Australia Death Index, 1787–1985. http://ancestry.co.uk.

Ancestry has assembled indexes from across much of Australia, but the information content is essentially the same as the governmental ones. In this case, age and parents' names are included but not a specific death place.

> Births index (CR). Australia. Queensland. 18 Dec 1883. MEABURN, Arthur Elliott. p. 10056. Reg. No. B031708. Collection: Australia, Births Index, 1788–1922. www.ancestry.com.

This Queensland record gives the full date of birth but still is not forthcoming about where in Queensland it took place.

New Zealand makes a fair amount of information available too, through a government website. Three examples follow. The formats are similar and very like those from Australia:

> Births index (CR). New Zealand. 1865. MEWBURN, James. Reg. 28846. https://bdmhistoricalrecords.dia.govt.nz/search.

Parents' given names are included.

> Deaths index (CR). New Zealand. 1866. MEWBURN [Newburn], Thomas William. Reg. 8056. https://bdmhistoricalrecords.dia.govt.nz/search.

Things are not always what are expected in these searches. A search on 1866 fails, while 1864 succeeds – but the registration number is given as 1866/8056. Purchase of the record would be needed to resolve the matter. Note that the indexes are not always correct in their name spelling.

> Marriages index (CR). New Zealand. 1894. MEWBURN, William and BARNES, Elizabeth. Reg. 857. https://bdmhistoricalrecords.dia.govt.nz/search.

This index record provides no detail beyond what appears in this reference.
  The major online data providers offer some material too.

> Burials. New Zealand. Wanganui, Rangiteki. 27 Jul 1966. MEWBURN, Sarah Ann. Collection: New Zealand, Cemetery Records, 1800–2007. www.ancestry.com.

Burial records can be found online, but many are published independently by local authorities so, for those, you need to know what the local authority is called.

Canadian material appears online in a patchy way, and its availability varies from province to province. There is a centralised facility in the form of Library and Archives Canada at: http://www.bac-lac.gc.ca/eng/discover/genealogy/Pages/introduction.aspx. However, their system is not always reliable when searching for ancestors, so other sources may be preferred.

> Births (CR). Canada. Stamford, Welland, Ontario. 06 Sep 1895. MEWBURN [Newcurer], John Stewart. MS929; Reel 129; Ref 032996. Collection: Ontario, Canada, Births, 1869–1913. http://search.ancestry.co.uk/.

Ontario is generally the best documented province. In this case, an image of the register page is available and shows that the accompanying transcription, which gives the name as Newcurer rather than Mewburn, is inaccurate. The reference is therefore to the image and not to the transcribed index entry.

> Baptisms index (PR). Canada. Charlottetown, Prince Edward Island. 22 Jul 1817 (birth 01 Mar 1817). NELSON, Wellington. Film no 1487764; image 02968. Collection: Prince Edward Island Baptism Card Index, 1721–1885. https://familysearch.org/ark:/61903/1:1:KCXJ-D4T.

This is given as an index record because, though the digitised image is available, it is itself the image of an index card.

> Deaths index (CR). Canada. North Vancouver, British Columbia. 08 Jul 1953. MEWBURN, Herman Lloyd Murray. Ref ID 53 09 007814; film no 2032875; image 02342. Collection: British Columbia Death Registrations, 1872–1986; 1992–1993. https://familysearch.org/ark:/61903/1:1:FLR8-SYN.

Some relatively modern information can also be found.

> Burials. Canada. Stamford, Ontario. 21 Sep 1867. MEWBURN, Arthur. Collection: Burial Records 1849-1931, St. John the Evangelist, Stamford, Ontario, Canada. Sec. A, p. 10.abt. http://www.nflibrary.ca/nfplindex/.

Information may be kept at a local level – in this case the Niagara Falls Public Library's website.

In the **USA** things are also organised largely on a state basis, often at county level. Records are commonly held in local courthouses and are being digitised and made available online in a fairly piecemeal fashion. Birth and death records are often not available before the late nineteenth or early twentieth century. *The Source*,[15] that great compendium for American genealogists, devotes only thirty or so of its 900+ pages to BMD records. Census returns, monumental inscriptions and newspaper items are often the best way to identify people from the USA when working online.

> Births (CR). USA. Port Huron, Michigan. 29 Aug 1908. MACDONALD, John Watt. Rec. No. 12769. State of Michigan, USA.

A reference to a record based on sight of the original certificate.

> Births index (CR). USA. Alameida, California. 14 Aug 1905. ALEXANDER, Muriel B. Collection: California Birth Index, 1905–1995. www.ancestry.com.

There are a few birth indexes available but the information given is sketchy. In this case, it also gives the mother's maiden name as being Young, but nothing more.

> Marriages index (CR). USA. Powhatan, Virginia. 20 Jan 1814. MEWBURN [Menburn], William and RANDOLPH, Sarah. Collection: Virginia, Marriages, 1785–1940 Transcription. www.findmypast.com.

A conventional reference but the image is not available so this is treated as an index entry. Because the transcription is known to be wrong, the index name is given in square brackets by the researcher.

> Deaths index (CR). USA. Virginia. Oct 1973 (birth 25 Aug 1925). MEWBORN, Larice. Social Security Number 226-22-3530. Collection: Social Security Death Index. www.findmypast.com.

The Social Security Death Index is a key source for American death and birth data when searching online.

Material from other parts of **Europe** can be treated in a similar generic fashion by using source types and collections. So, for example:

> Births (CR). Poland. Kraków, Malopolskie. 08 Sep 1874. FISCHER, Jetta. Film 1201162; page 52; entry 516. Collection: Matrykuła, 1798-1989. Gmina Żydowska, Kraków. http://www.jri-poland.org.

In fact, this reference conceals a complex web for the researcher. The source is on an LDS film which is found in their Polish collection. At the time of this birth that part of Poland was ruled by Austria, so strictly speaking the records are Austrian and were created by Austrian administrations. This record has not been indexed by the LDS so cannot be found in searches on FamilySearch (some others can). Instead it is identified in the Jewish Records Indexing – Poland database (and via the www.Jewishgen. org website) where it points you to the correct LDS film. The collection title is the name for the material as it is catalogued by the LDS. Finally, such birth records were registered by the Catholic Church. They did not accept the validity of Jewish marriages so, rather disconcertingly, all Jewish births are recorded as illegitimate. The records may be written in a mix of German and Polish.

> Marriages (CR). France. Toulouse, Haute-Garonne. 28 Sep 1853. COLOMBIES, Jeanne Marguerite and MEDARD, Adelaide Valentine. Collection: France, Haute-Garonne, Toulouse, état civil, 1792–1893. https://familysearch.org/ark:/61903/1:1:Q23N-Z2GV.

A conventional reference from a record image, though, of course, the record is in French.

EXAMPLES: FAMILY BIBLES AND DIARIES

Primary source material may not always have such formal origins as church and state records. Members of a family often record BMD events, and the documents they use can be crucial in determining family relationships and linkages. The 'what' and 'who' portions of your reference can remain the same as in the examples above (though without qualifiers such as CR or PR), while the 'where' becomes an identification of the document.

> Baptisms. England. Eston, Yorkshire. 22 Mar 1764. MEWBURN, Wm. In: Mewburn, William. *Diary and Accounts, 1761–1816, Eston and Ormesby.* Image 2. Toronto, Canada: Archives of Ontario.

An example from an eighteenth-century diary. The information has been taken from scanned images of the original (two pages per image). The actual document is more a set of farm accounts than a diary, though interleaved with diverse items that the author thought worth recording.

> Births. USA. North Carolina. 11 Mar 1832. MEWBORN, Mary. Collection: Mewborn Family Bible Records. p. 4. Raleigh, North Carolina: State Archives of North Carolina. http://digital.ncdcr.gov/cdm/ref/collection/p15012coll1/id/6483.

A reference from a set of family bibles now digitised and available online.

Referencing census returns

Census returns that identify individuals are arguably another great form of vital record (so BMDC is often used as an alternative acronym for the key genealogical records) and are hugely beneficial in helping the researcher identify family structures. A generic style can be used that will cover most censuses from most countries.

Elements in the reference are:

- Source type. [Census returns]
- Country. [this always qualifies the source type as specific formats of record vary from place to place]
- Place. [for example, parish, county]
- Date of census. [the day when it was due, if possible]
- NAME, given name(s). [person being enumerated in the census]
- Record identifier. [this varies by administration but should include the Registration District and other things such as Series or Class; Piece; Folio; and Page or the ScotlandsPeople data number. There is a Schedule number for the 1911 English/Welsh census and a Form number for the 1901 and 1911 Irish censuses]
- Collection: Name of collection. [if the item was found within a database with multiple collections, then give the name of the collection. You do not need to do this for ScotlandsPeople since it is the only online source for original source images]
- URL. [if the item was found online. See the URL guidelines for details]

Notes on elements

There are censuses that do little more than count numbers of people in various locations. These can be useful in providing contextual information when writing family histories. Our principal concern for genealogical purposes is, however, with those censuses that identify individuals, and maybe also their addresses. That type of census is typically carried out by a governmental body.

The referencing style described here is not intended to be used for unofficial counts that create records we call census substitutes – for example the *status animarum* prepared by Roman Catholic priests to identify members of their flock.

Not all the elements that can be used in a reference will be needed (or available), depending upon the country and year of the census you are referring to. Remember that the main purpose of references is to enable your reader to find the source again; the elements in the references below have been included with that in mind. Note, however, that it is rarely the case that the archival references can be used in online searches.

Because we cite in relation to an individual, that person should be named in the reference. If they are not, then the reference becomes an uninformative generic thing, typically pointing to a whole page of entries and offering no clue as to who is relevant on that page. This is true, of course, for most parish records. The same needs to be done, therefore, with census records to provide consistency of approach and relevance to the reader.

The person who is named is the one we are referring to in our text, not necessarily the principal householder.

It is also useful, following the belt-and-braces principle, to include the official identifier or coding scheme that points to the archived census record. The structure and system of identification varies between administrations and over time, so those mentioned here are simply typical. You may find records from places that use different terminology.

The exact date when the census was conducted is significant. It is helpful to know, as it assists in understanding why some people are, or are not, in the census. They may be missing if they were born after the census date, or died before it. The date can help to narrow down the timing of these other life events.

Take care, though, not to read too much into the date. Even if the record is supposed to reflect status on the census date, by the time enumeration actually took place, the householders' recollections may not have been perfect and they may not have made a good job of recording in the first place. The enumeration process sometimes extended over a significant period. The first US Federal census in 1790 was scheduled to take nine months but was extended until 1 March 1792.

Here are the dates for some censuses (note that Canada did not exist, other than as a group of separate colonies, until 1867, so censuses before that are partial):

Census Year	Date UK	Date USA Federal	Date NSW Australia	Date Canada (partial before 1871)
1790		02 Aug 1790		
1800		04 Aug 1800		
1810		06 Aug 1810		
1820		07 Aug 1820		
1828			Nov 1828	
1830		01 Jun 1830		
1840		01 Jun 1840		
1841	06 Jun 1841		02 Mar 1841	
1850		01 Jun 1850		
1851	30 Mar 1851			11 Jan 1851
1852				12 Jan 1852 (Canada W&E)
1860		01 Jun 1860		
1861	07 Apr 1861			13 Jan 1861 (East & West) 15 Aug 1861 (New Brunswick)
1868		21 Oct 1868		
1870		01 Jun 1870		
1871	02 Apr 1871			02 Apr 1871
1880		01 Jun 1880		
1881	03 Apr 1881			04 Apr 1881
1891	05 Apr 1891		04 Apr 1891	06 Apr 1891
1900		01 Jun 1900		
1901	31 Mar 1901		31 Mar 1901	31 Mar 1901

1906				1906 (Manitoba, Saskatchewan, Alberta)
1910		15 Apr 1910		
1911	02 Apr 1911			01 Jun 1911
1916				1916 (Manitoba, Saskatchewan, Alberta)
1920		01 Jan 1920		
1921				01 Jun 1921
1930		01 Apr 1930		
1939	29 Sep 1939			
1940		01 Apr 1940		

Note. The 1939 entry for the UK is for the National Register, which was not officially a census.

EXAMPLES

> Census returns index. Scotland. Kingsbarns, Fife. 06 Jun 1841. ANDERSON, Alexander. 441/00 001/00 007. http://www.scotlandspeople.gov.uk.

The ScotlandsPeople data number includes codes for the registration district (441/00), enumeration district (001/00) as well as page number information (007) so these do not have to be spelled out in the reference. The place information and person's name are all that are needed to enable the system to be searched to re-examine the original image. This has been listed as an index record since it is referencing just the result of a search in ScotlandsPeople. The image has not been accessed. Note that the reference is not absolutely specific but points to two Alexander Andersons, at the same place, one aged 20 and the other 0 – a reason, perhaps, to pay for sight of the image.

> Census returns. England. All Saints, Southampton, Hampshire. 30 Mar 1851. YOULDEN, John K. HO107; piece 1669; folio 854; p. 51. Collection: 1851 England, Wales & Scotland Census Image. http://www.findmypast.co.uk.

In this English record, the place identification is set out a little more explicitly. This is not labelled as a transcription or an index since the record image is provided as well as a transcription.

> Census returns. Scotland. Latheron, Caithness. 02 Apr 1871. BRUCE, Donald. RD 038; ED 12; p. 4.

This census record was viewed on microfilm at a family history centre so there is no question of including a URL. Latheron in Caithness is the registration district and the author has chosen to spell out the codes rather than show it as the GROS data number. That is an acceptable choice.

Census returns index. Wales. Loughor, Llanelly, Carmarthenshire. 05 Apr 1891. JONES, Griffith. RG12; piece 4491; folio 13; p. 19. Collection: England & Wales Census, 1891. https://familysearch.org/ark:/61903/1:1:4PQR-5T2.

This is just a transcription but full details are present that will enable the original document to be traced. The fixed URL should bring your reader to the specific page within FamilySearch and at that point there is a link to the record image (on FindMyPast) so in principle there is no need to rely on the transcription. It would be better practice to provide a reference to the image, though this FamilySearch reference has the benefit of being free.

Census returns. England. Bayton, Worcestershire. 31 Mar 1901. AVERILL [Avriett], Nathaniel. ED 12; piece 2515; folio 142; p. 4. Collection: 1901 England Census. http://ancestry.co.uk.

In this case Bayton is the civil parish and Worcestershire is the county given in the census. This one can be tricky to find as the name has been transcribed as Avriett so we include both spellings to help the reader.

Census returns index. Scotland. Dumfries, Dumfriesshire. 31 Mar 1901. ADAMSON, Christopher. RN 821; ED 13; SN 167. Collection: 1910 Scotland Census [transcription]. http://ancestry.co.uk.

The ED number has been included here as this is an Ancestry transcription (with the inevitable uncertainty over completeness) with no associated image and thus there is no ScotlandsPeople number to add. Ancestry has not shown the page number in this Scottish census so you cannot add it into the reference.

Census returns. England. Aston, Warwickshire. 02 Apr 1911. AARON, Francis. RD 385; PN 18210; ED 21; SN 101. Collection: 1911 England & Wales Census Collection Image. http://www.findmypast.co.uk.

The 1911 English/Welsh census reference provides additional information and enhanced reliability since we can view the schedule as filled in by the householder as well as a transcription. 385 is the registration district number; Aston is the name of the registration district.

Census returns. England. Camberwell, London. 29 Sep 1939. FISHER, Malcolm G. RD 25-1; ED AECN. Collection: 1939 Register Image. http://www.findmypast.co.uk.

Strictly speaking this is not a census but is an entry from the 1939 National Register compiled to provide the UK government with an accurate picture of the state of the nation at the outbreak of war. RD and ED Letter Code can be found on the form image. Since a copy of the image is always provided by FindMyPast, the transcription, which is also available, should not be cited.

> Census returns. Ireland. Grosvenor Square, Rathmines and Rathgar West, Dublin. 02 Apr 1911. WILSON, Elizabeth Jenning. FN 14. Collection: Census of Ireland 1901/1911 and Census fragments and substitutes 1821–51. http://www.census.nationalarchives.ie/search/.

The basic topographical divisions for the Irish census are: Townland or Street; District Electoral Division; County. This is how search results are arranged in the National Archives of Ireland's database and the pattern we've chosen to follow in the reference example above.

Other administrations will use different formats for their data collection forms, and will gather some different items of data reflecting current governmental concerns. Nevertheless, a similar approach to those above can be taken to composing a reference.

> Census returns. Canada. Stamford, Ontario. 02 April 1871. MEWBURN, Francis. DN 19-j; p. 30. Collection: 1871 Census of Canada. http://ancestry.co.uk.

This is from the first national census in Canada and our general format has been used successfully. Here we have a District Number and a sub-district letter to identify the schedule.

> Census returns. Canada West. Stamford, Welland. 12 Jan 1852. MEWBURN, John. Sub-dist. 382. p.10d, 11a, (21). Collection: 1851 Census, Ontario and Quebec. http://www.automatedgenealogy.com/.

This is prior to Canada becoming a nation, hence Canada West (later the basis for Ontario). Automated Genealogy is a free source dedicated to transcribing census records. Note that though this is the 1851 census, it didn't actually take place until early 1852. These things happen.

> Census returns. United States. Sullivan, Indiana. 01 Jun 1860. MEWBURN, Simon. Film 803298. Image 00402. Collection: United States Census 1860. https://familysearch.org/ark:/61903/1:1:M4NV-QH5.

This is a US Federal census. Here FamilySearch provides both a digitised image and a fixed URL.

The unexpected can occur. The law in England requires that a person be recorded at only one place on the night of the census. However, things don't always work out quite like that, as the following two entries show.

Census returns. England. Military, India. 02 Apr 1911. MEWBURN, [Newburn] Simon William. RG14; piece 34991. Collection: 1911 England Census. www.ancestry.com.

Simon was an army officer and is listed as a member of his regiment. He wasn't in India, he was simply destined to go there. The listing does say, however, that he was absent on the night and, indeed, he can also be found at the family home:

Census returns. England. St Margaret & St John, London. 02 Apr 1911. MEWBURN, Simon William Richmond. RG14; piece 00488. Collection: 1911 England, Wales & Scotland Census Image. www.findmypast.com.

Just to wrap up the preceding sections, a lot of space has been devoted to BMDC records since these are so important to genealogical research. A variety of other nominal records are available, however, and need to be exploited to fill out details of peoples' lives and their histories. The principal types follow.

Referencing electoral listings

Various forms of list – for example, poll books, rolls, registers and lists – are used to keep track of those people who have voted or are eligible to vote in local or national elections. Early ones list only men, but as suffrage was granted they steadily developed into relatively comprehensive registers of the adult population (with some legal exclusions).

A great benefit is that they typically provide the registered address for each person. In earlier listings that would be for the property that qualified them for voting purposes; an address where the person actually lived might also be given. The listings are, of course, published at regular intervals so an individual's changes of address can be traced, sometimes over a substantial period.

Another benefit is that adult children sometimes appear on the roll at the same address as their parents, once they reach voting age. That helps in identifying candidate children, where birth records are unavailable, and provides a clue to their approximate year of birth (you have to know the voting age at the time of the listing; over time voting ages have been dropping). This can be convenient when researching relatively recent families in administrations where there are timing restrictions on the release of birth data.

Electoral listings are generally public documents that are kept current (give or take the duration of the electoral cycle). However, they do not specify relationships so care must be taken over accepting an implication of linkage. Additional supporting evidence should be sought (the extra person with the same surname could be any family member – sibling, cousin etc. – or even none at all).

Elements in the reference are:

- Source type. [Electoral listings]
- Country.
- Place. [typically, parish and county]
- Date of item. [in most cases, this will be the year the listing was issued. Typically, the information will have been gathered some months before]
- NAME, given name(s). [person eligible]
- Registered number. [if applicable]
- Page number. [in the listing, if available]
- Collection: Name of collection. [if the item was found within a database with multiple collections, then give the name of the collection]
- URL. [if the item was found online. See the URL guidelines for details]

Notes on elements

These are another form of nominal record and, like census returns, they enable us to plot the movements of individuals across significant periods of their lives since they specify the dwelling place, or place of entitlement to vote.

The structure is chosen to mimic that used for censuses.

EXAMPLES

Electoral listings. England. Pontop, Durham. 1675. MEBORNE, Anth. Esq. p. 24. Collection: UK, Poll Books and Electoral Registers, 1538–1893. www. ancestry.com.

An early Poll Book entry (and at that time it also shows how votes were cast). Anthony was recognised as one of the gentry, hence the 'Esq'.

Electoral listings. England. Islington, London. 1831. HUMES, Patrick Joseph. No. 1529. p. 646. Collection: London, England, Electoral Registers, 1832-1965. www.ancestry.com.

A conventional register entry. However, the record is from 1831 though the Collection title suggests it runs from 1832.

Electoral listings. England. Wooton, Oxfordshire. 1862. BLOUNT, Walter Aston. No. 4407. p. 131. Collection: UK, Poll Books and Electoral Registers, 1538–1893. www.ancestry.com.

An entry in respect of a farm property that provides the holder's right to vote, though the owner's address is given as Ovington Square, London.

Electoral listings. England. St George Hanover Square, Middlesex. 1863. BLOUNT, Walter Aston. MR/PEO/1863/11/3. London Metropolitan Archive, London, England. Collection: London, England, Overseer Returns, 1863–1894. http://www.ancestry.co.uk.

Walter Blount again. In this case, the 'Collection: London, England, Overseer Returns, 1863–1894' is the name of the Ancestry collection within which this record was found. Information on the repository (code, name and place) was included in the Ancestry record so is included here.

> Electoral listings. England. St George Hanover Square, Westminster. 1864. BLOUNT, Walter Aston. No. 1708. p. 46. Collection: London, England, Electoral Registers, 1832–1965. www.ancestry.com.

An entry for the man in the example above in the Electoral Register a year later. It is often possible to track people over a number of years with these records.
Variations on the theme are found in many other countries.

> Electoral listings. New Zealand. Auckland Central, Auckland. 1928. MEWBURN, Millard James. No. 6522. p. 132. Collection: New Zealand, Electoral Rolls, 1853–1981. www.ancestry.com.

An example from New Zealand where the listings take a similar form to those from the UK, though called Rolls. However, check the next example.

> Electoral listings. Australia. Oakleigh, Henty, Victoria. 1931. MEWBURN, Millard James. No. 7306. p. 123. Collection: Australia, Electoral Rolls, 1903–1980. www.ancestry.com.

A slightly later example from Victoria, Australia showing the same man as in the example above – evidently having migrated from New Zealand.

> Electoral listings. Canada. Coast Chilcotin, British Columbia. 1974. COURTE, Victor. No. 6889. Ref. 98223. p. 2. Collection: Canada, Voters Lists, 1935–1980. www.ancestry.com.

A Canadian example, titled a little differently as a Voters List.

> Electoral listings. USA. San Francisco, California. 1868. MEABURN, John James. Voting No. 25166. Reg. No. 26590. Collection: California, Voters Registers, 1866-1898. www.ancestry.com.

And one from the USA known as the 'Great Register'.

Referencing directories and professional lists

The first commercial directory in the UK was published in the seventeenth century. They became more popular in the eighteenth and became almost universally available in the nineteenth. As well as listing people by trade they often listed the local gentry and notable residents, and in consequence are a valuable resource to the genealogist. They are contemporary records so we treat them as primary, though with caution since publication could be some time after the data gathering.

We can include under this heading more specialist publications such as lists for professionals in the law, or the church, when those were compiled as books for sale.

Elements in the reference are:

- Source type. [Directory entries]
- Country.
- Place. [typically, town and county if relevant]
- Year or year range.
- NAME, given name(s). [of person listed]
- *Title.* [in *italics* since we treat directories in much the same way as monographs. If this is an authored book then it may be preceded by 'In: Author name']
- Place of publication: Name of publisher.
- Page number. [if available]
- Collection: Name of collection. [if the item was found within a database with multiple collections, then give the name of the collection]
- URL. [if the item was found online. See the URL guidelines for details]

EXAMPLES

Directory entries. England. Plymouth, Devonshire. BARRABALL, Ann. 1902. *Kelly's Directory of Devon, 1902*. London: Kelly's Directories Limited. p. 552. http://archive.org/details/kellysdirectoryo00londuoft.

Kelly's is, of course, one of the most successful and ubiquitous of directories.

Directory entries. England. 1868. HOTHAM, John Hallett. *Crockford's Clerical Directory*. 4th Issue. London: Horace Cox. p. 337. www.ancestry.com.

Crockford's provides a brief history for each entrant, which can be genealogically valuable. The current Crockford's offers an online subscription service at: https://www.crockford.org.uk.

Directory entries. Scotland. 1925. RUSSELL, James. In: Scott, Hew. *Fasti Ecclesiae Scoticanae; the Succession of Ministers in the Church of Scotland from the Reformation*. Edinburgh: Oliver and Boyd. p. 204.

Fasti is the great Scottish catalogue of ministers. This has an identified author so this time we have treated it as a monograph. Each entry gives a potted biography with family details so, like Crockford's, is invaluable to the genealogist. Much of the content in this kind of publication is derived and not of the moment so, though invaluable, is not primary and needs to be treated with appropriate caution.

Hew Scott was the original creator. After his time, the work was continued as a committee effort. Some of the committee efforts were less painstaking but, bizarrely, to begin with were published in the name of the deceased Hew. Take extra care over the later material.

Directory entries. Scotland. Dundee, Fife. 1890–91. BLACKLAWS, John. *Dundee directory*. Dundee: James P. Mathew and Co. p. 147. http://digital.nls. uk/85774477.

Many directories were local productions. Note that dating for them could be slightly imprecise and, naturally, the material had been gathered some time in advance of the publication date. Do not assume that a place in a directory meant that the person was still alive by the publication date.

Directory entries. England. London. 1824. MEWBURN, Bowyer. *Clarke's New List; being a list of all the Judges and Officers of the different Courts of Justice: Counsel, Special Pleaders, Conveyancers; and a Complete and Accurate list of the Certificated Attorneys, Notaries &c. in England and Wales with the London Agents to the County Attornies*. London: J. & T. W. Clarke, p. 94.

A Law List. Lists of this kind started to be produced as greater professionalism and the requirement for qualification became accepted as a necessary prerequisite for entry and entitlement to practise.

Directory entries. England. Kensington, London. 1925. DOUGLAS, Ena. *Phone Book London Surnames A–Z*. Chelsea, London. p. 320. London: Post Office. Collection: British Phone Books, 1880–1984. www.ancestry.com.

Phone books started quite early though the number of entries back in 1880 was small. An additional benefit is that addresses are included. People may also appear under businesses that are run in their names. A precise title and publisher's details may be difficult to discover. For interest, check out the BT Digital Archives: http://www. digitalarchives.bt.com/web/arena.

Referencing membership lists

Organisations that people have been part of generally held lists of their members. Some are fairly uninformative, but others include addresses, and some may include parents' names and even the person's history within the organisation. We can include school admissions in this general category as well as participation in clubs and societies. Unlike directories these were not primarily intended for publication.

Elements in the reference are:

- Source type. [Membership listings]
- Country. [if appropriate]
- Year or year range.
- NAME, given name(s). [of person listed]
- *Title.* [in *italics.* If this is an authored book then it may be preceded by 'In: Author name']
- Place of publication: Name of publisher.
- Page number.
- Collection: Name of collection. [if the item was found within a database with multiple collections, then give the name of the collection]
- URL. [if the item was found online. See the URL guidelines for details]

EXAMPLES ───

Membership listings. 1931. CROOK, Thomas Mewburn. *The Savage Club List of Members.* London: The Savage Club. Collection: Thomas Mewburn Crook Fonds, Box 6. Leeds: Henry Moore Institute.

A traditional list for a London gentlemens' club, the list being held at a specialist archive.

Membership listings. 2017. McCABE, Tahitia. *Register of Qualified Genealogists,* website. www.qualifiedgenealogists.org.

This is a relatively simple listing published online. It is for an international organisation so Country is not appropriate. Often listings will not have been published and will be referenced almost like private communications.

Membership listings. England. 1781. ANDERSON, John. *Freemasonry Membership Registers; Description: Register of Admissions: Country and Foreign,* Vol. II, folios 1–649. London: Library and Museum of Freemasonry. p. 254. Collection: England, United Grand Lodge of England Freemason Membership Registers, 1751–1921. www.ancestry.com.

A purer form of membership list. Lists will exist for similar organisations such as the Rotary Club, Oddfellows or Elks. The names of other members provide an insight into social relationships.

Membership listings. England. 1808. MEWBURN, Francis. *A List of the Members of the Royal College of Surgeons in London, Who do not reside or practise in or within seven miles of the City of London.* London, Lincoln's Inn Fields: The Royal College of Surgeons Library.

This is a slightly odd example as it is not openly published (so is not a directory) but is maintained within the library (and is not stamped with a shelfmark). It could equally be cited as a publication by the Royal College of Surgeons with their name appearing in the 'author' position. Either way the source would be findable.

Increasingly, old-established organisations choose to publish compilations of their membership over the years. Sometimes the members are listed in histories of the organisation. These can be referenced as membership listings when pointing to an individual, or as books under the name of the compiler or editor. Here are a couple of examples. These, however, are not contemporary listings so are secondary in nature and must be treated with appropriate caution.

> Membership listings. England. 1844. MEWBURN, Chilton. In: Gardiner, Robert Barlow. 1884. *The Admission Registers of St. Paul's School, from 1748–1867*. London: George Bell and Sons. p. 311. http://www.archive.org/details/admissionregist00gardgoog.

Details of registrations contained within a book that purports to be a compilation derived from the original registers. Alternatively, this could be referenced as an entry in a book.

> Membership listings. Scotland. 1862. CHRYSTALL, James. In: Gordon, George. 2000[?]. *The Shore Porters' Society of Aberdeen 1498–1998*. Aberdeen: The Shore Porters' Society. pp. 173–174.

The book is a history (an anniversary publication; the first 109 pages were originally published in 1969!), but it contains a comprehensive set of members' biographies in a sixty-five-page Personalia section. The book does not give its publication date.

Referencing service records

When people engage in any form of public service their spell within it tends to be thoroughly documented. The commonest field for such records is military service, but other examples are police, lifeboat or fire service. The records are akin to an employment or human resources history so, in principle, similar records might be found for any organisation. In this case, though, our focus is on official records.

These can generally be attributed to the government department or organisation that the people were attached to. If they are official records they are likely to end up in public archives where the name of the responsible, or depositing, organisation is generally used to identify them in the archiving process. In the UK, military service records from the First World War and the Second World War will appear in War Office deposits. The material can cover a diverse range of types of record.

Elements in the reference are:

- Source type (name of service). [Service records, qualified by army, police etc.]
- Country.
- Archival collection name. [e.g. War Office, Department of Defense. These records are likely to be organised into collections of this kind]
- Name of record type. [attestation, discharge, medal card and so on]
- Date record created.
- NAME, given name(s). [of the serving person]
- Service identifier. [if available; varies with context; may indicate a part of the organisation where the person served (Regiment, for example); may include an identification number]
- Collection: Name of collection. [if the item was found within a database with multiple collections, then give the name of the collection]
- URL. [if the item was found online. See the URL guidelines for details]

EXAMPLES

Service records (army). England. War Office (Great Britain). Short Service Attestation. 26 Apr 1915. CHALONER, George. Cheshire Regiment. Regimental Number: 26082. Collection: British Army WWI Service Records, 1914–1920. http://www.ancestry.co.uk.

A considerable range of War Office records exists but the combination of the record title and the name of the collection it appears in should make it findable.

Service records (army). England. War Office (Great Britain). Record of Service Paper. 10 Jun 1918. CAPPER, Frederick. Machine Gun Guards. Service number: 6936. Collection: British Army WWI Pension Records 1914–1920. http://www.ancestry.co.uk.

This demonstrates the range and diversity of materials maintained within a single government department.

Service records (army). England. War Office (Great Britain). Army Service Records: Discharge. 08 May 1852. FISHER, Henry. Service Number: 3084. Collection: WO97 Chelsea Pensioners British Army Service Records 1760–1913. Kew, London: The National Archives.

This record has been inspected directly at the archive so has no URL but includes the TNA WO (War Office) series that it belongs to.

Service records (army). England. War Office (Great Britain). Service Medal and Award Rolls Index, First World War. Medal Card. CHALONER, George. Corps: Cheshire Regiment. Regiment No: 26082. Reference: WO 372/4/67866. Kew, London: The National Archives.

Another example of a War Office record within the corresponding WO series at TNA.

> Service records (army). England. War Office (Great Britain). Roll of Individuals entitled to the Victory Medal and British War Medal. CHALONER, George. Regimental number: 26082. Collection: UK WWI Service Medal and Award Rolls, 1914–1920. http://www.ancestry.co.uk.

The same record as the one before would be attributed slightly differently when using the information findable on an online site.

> Service records (army). England. War Office (Great Britain). War Deaths, Army Other Ranks (1914–1921). 24 Jul 1915. AGER, Percy A. Suffolk Regiment. Regimental Number: 9109. Collection: British Nationals armed forces deaths 1796–2005. http://findmypast.co.uk.

A typical example of listing for a soldier's death.

> Service records (police). Canada. 14 Aug 1966. CARTER, Leslie James. Regimental No. 9505. Collection: RCMP Graves Database. http://www.rcmpgraves.com/database/search.html.

An unusual example where, what might be expected to be a record of memorial inscriptions, incorporates a database covering the complete service record of members of the Canadian Mounties.

> Service records index (air force). Australia. Melbourne, Victoria. MEWBURN, Thomas Vere. RAAF Enlistment. 1939–45. 438864. Collection: Australia WWII Military Service Records, 1939–1945. www.ancestry.com.

An index entry to a Royal Australian Air Force (RAAF) record for the Second World War (hence the lack of an exact date).

> Service records (army). Australia. Boorowa, New South Wales. 16 Sep 1915. MEWBURN, Arthur Allen. AIF Attestation Paper of Persons Enlisted for Service Abroad. Collection: Australia WWI Service Records, 1914–1920. www.ancestry.com.

A First World War record for the Australian Imperial Force (AIF). The image is provided so the exact date of attestation can be given.

> Service records index (army). Australia. Paddington, New South Wales. MEWBURN, Horace Vivian. CMF Enlistment. 1939–45. N445110. Collection: All Australia, World War II Military Service Records, 1939–1945. www.ancestry.com.

An index to a Second World War record for the Australian Citizen Military Forces – a militia operating within Australia and its territories.

Referencing testamentary records

Various kinds of record may relate to how a person's wishes or assumed wishes are handled at or around the time of death. We call these, generically, testamentary records; they include such things as wills, testaments, inventories administrations and probate. A single style can be used to reference any of them.

Elements in the reference are:

- Source type. [Testamentary records]
- Country.
- Place. [Parish, county where the will was written, if available]
- Date of record. [the date of confirmation, probate, registration, etc.]
- NAME, given name(s). [of moribund or deceased person]
- Type of item. [Will, Probate, Testament testamentar, Inventory, Administration, etc.]
- (Will – Will date. Place). [Optional. When and where the will was written]
- Death date. [Optional. If given]
- Reference code(s). [if applicable. This refers to any archival codes referring to that source, collection and/or repository]
- Repository name, [if applicable] Repository location. [if applicable]
- Collection: Name of collection. [if the item was found within a database with multiple collections, then give the name of the collection]
- URL. [if the item was found online. See the URL guidelines for details]

Notes on elements

The names given to things that are testamentary differ from country to country and from jurisdiction to jurisdiction.

The date should be the date for the record. Most often that is likely to be the probate or administration date. Wills are often found as part of the probate or administration record but it is the record date that should be given. If the will is dated, that date is given separately (with the place it was written).

Strictly speaking, the inclusion of a separate will date and death date is unnecessary to the reference but it can help the reader, especially if some dates are far apart.

EXAMPLES

Testamentary records. England. Lanchester, Durham. 11 Apr 1573. MEBURNE, Jhon. Probate. (Will – 01 Sep 1572). Durham. Collection: Prerogative Court of Canterbury: Will Registers. DPRI/1/1573/M2/1. Durham: Durham University.

Images for many Durham wills are now available on FindMyPast. This one is not.

> Testamentary records. England. Bristol, Gloucestershire. 03 Apr 1635. BLOUNT, Robert. Probate. (Will – 17 Feb 1634. City of Bristol). Collection: Prerogative Court of Canterbury: Will Registers. PROB 11/167/363. Kew, England: The National Archives. http://discovery.nationalarchives.gov.uk/SearchUI/details/D868358?uri=D868358-details.

The URL takes you to a point on TNA's website where a fee can be paid and a scanned image of the will downloaded.

> Testamentary records. Wales. Llanfairfechan, Caernarfon. 10 Feb 1806. JONES, John. Will and Grant of Administration. (Will – 29 Apr 1805). B1806-63 National Library of Wales, Aberystwyth. Collection: Bangor Probate Records, 1576-1858. http://hdl.handle.net/10107/575311.

In this case, the URL (a Permalink) takes you to a point on the National Library of Wales website where a scanned image of the will can be viewed.

> Testamentary records index. England. Principal Registry. 21 Mar 1861. CAMPBELL, Ann. (Death – 04 Feb 1861. Pembroke Docks, Pembrokeshire). Collection: England & Wales, National Probate Calendar (Index of Wills and Administrations), 1858–1966. p. 10. http://www.ancestry.co.uk.

This is for a printed probate calendar entry found within a digitised copy of the Calendar of Confirmations available on Ancestry.co.uk. This information is an official summary of key details from the will and probate proceedings. It is both a derived record and an index entry, though carrying most of the essential detail.

> Testamentary records. Scotland. Aberdeen, Aberdeenshire. 22 Aug 1889. REID, or M'DONALD or STEWART, Margaret. Settlement. (Will – 01 Jul 1881. Alford, Aberdeenshire). Aberdeen Sheriff Court Wills. SC1/37/104. http://www.scotlandspeople.gov.uk.

This brings joy to the heart of any genealogist. Here we get a maiden surname (McDonald – the apostrophe is a transcriber's oddity) and two married names setting out key elements in the life of the lady. Admittedly, the sequence is not right since it should go Reid, Stewart, McDonald, but that is a quibble in the midst of such riches.

> Testamentary records. Scotland. Glasgow, Lanarkshire. 23 Mar 1869. MONTGOMERIE, Mathew. Trust disposition and settlement. (Will – 04 Jun 1867). Glasgow Sheriff Court Wills. SC36/51/55. http://www.scotlandspeople.gov.uk.

An example of another kind of testamentary document.

Testamentary records. Scotland. Llandudno, Carnarvon. 02 Dec 1885. NEWNES, Thomas Mold. Copy administration of effects. Non-Scottish Court. (Death – 21 Dec 1884). SC70/6/29. http://www.scotlandspeople.gov.uk.

Owning property in multiple administrations can lead to records appearing in each of them. Thomas was living in Wales at the time of his death but records appear at the Edinburgh Sherriff Court (there are actually four sets of records available).

Sometimes testamentary information is found not in a testament, but in a note retained among lawyers' records. These records are sometimes known as protocol books and can contain information valuable to the family historian on many topics, wherever someone needed legal assistance. For example:

Testamentary records. Scotland. 1554. CRYCHTOUNE, Elizabeth. Memorandum of conveyance. In: Angus, William, ed. 1914. *Grote, Gilbert (1552–1573) Protocol Book*. p. 3. Edinburgh: Scottish Record Society. https://archive.org/stream/ scottishrecordso31scotuoft/scottishrecordso31scotuoft_djvu.txt.

All sorts of other things appear in protocol books so they may be cited just as monographs with the appropriate page reference. In this case we are treating an entry as a testamentary record substitute.

Referencing monumental inscriptions

Burial grounds and churches provide a feast of information to the researcher through monumental inscriptions (MIs) aimed at providing lasting memorials to people and often to family members linked with them. (In case of any confusion these are inscriptions on monuments not inscriptions that are monumental!) This category can be more broadly drawn though, to include war memorials, 'Blue Plaques',[16] rolls of honour in schools, universities and workplaces and other inscriptions in or attached to buildings or structures everywhere that celebrate worthy individuals.

Particularly in the case of graveyards, there may be published booklets containing transcriptions of the MIs. Bear in mind that the presence of a stone does not guarantee that there is a burial there – it may literally be just a memorial.

These are not primary records. Monumental inscriptions may be created some time after the people they mention have died – sometimes many years later. The date when the memorial was established may be uncertain and the identity of the informant is rarely known, so the quality of the data can be suspect. Beyond that the carver can make errors. Beyond that still, time and weather take their toll and accurate transcription may be an issue.

Particular care needs to be taken over the use of transcribed and published MIs and they need to be given their own health warnings. They are just transcriptions, and they are transcriptions of inscriptions that come with their own warnings. Even worse, early publications usually focused on just the 'important' people in a graveyard and typically used a range of curious abbreviations for the elements of the inscription. Even modern publications need to be checked to see how completely they have carried out the task.

Referencing, though, is generally less of an issue.

Elements in the reference are:

- Source type. [monumental inscriptions]
- Country.
- Place. [church name, parish, county, etc.]
- Date of death. [if referring to one person]
- NAME, given name(s). [of deceased person. Possibly just the family name if citing a group memorial]
- In: [give details of the transcriber's name (and date of transcription if transcribed personally) and of the publication and publisher, if applicable, and the page number for the entry, if relevant]
- Collection: Name of collection. [if the item was found within a database with multiple collections, then give the name of the collection]
- URL. [if the item was found online. See the URL guidelines for details]

EXAMPLES

For monumental inscriptions coming from a publication:

Monumental inscriptions. Scotland. Cupar Old Parish Churchyard, Cupar, Fife. 21 Mar 1861. CAMPBELL, Ann. In: Fife Family History Society. 2004. *Fifeshire monumental inscriptions (pre-1855), vol. 3. The north east parishes.* Edinburgh: Scottish Genealogy Society. p. 135.

A typical example of a modern published set of transcriptions.

Monumental inscriptions. England. Swaffam High Parish Churchyard, Lower Swaffam, Norfolk. BRERETON family. In: Norfolk Family History Society. 2012. *East Norfolk monumental inscriptions*, vol. 14. Norwich: Norfolk Family History Society. p. 204.

This is for a family stone with dates for many individuals and this page gives the transcription for the entire family.

Monumental inscriptions. Scotland. Cowie, Kincardineshire. 06 Mar 1863, BROWN, Thomas. Entry 148. In: Mitchell, Alison, ed. 1999. *Pre-1855 Gravestone Inscriptions in Kincardineshire.* Edinburgh: Scottish Genealogy Society. p. 177.

This is an example where highly abbreviated transcriptions are provided. The entry reads:

> '1863. Thos Brown tent Burnorachie d 6.3.1863 60, w Mary Spark 19.6.1866
> 60, da Elspet 13.12.1925 90'

Nevertheless, it is highly informative, telling us that Thomas was a tenant farmer and giving us death dates and ages at death for him, his wife and a daughter. However, it is possible that the stone was not raised until after the death of the daughter so the information needs to be treated with caution.

For monumental inscriptions coming from a researcher:

> Monumental inscriptions. Scotland. Cupar Old Parish Churchyard, Cupar, Fife. 21
> Mar 1861. CAMPBELL, Ann. Transcribed by Peter Jones, 16 February 2012.

Here we have an example of a monumental inscription where the researcher has looked at it personally and captured the information on it.

> Monumental inscriptions. England. Acomb, Northumberland. ARMSTRONG,
> Jane. Plaque within Acomb House. Transcribed by Ian G. Macdonald. 2011.

In this case, there is no public access but there is adequate information about the location of the inscription.

For monumental inscriptions coming from a website:

> Monumental inscriptions. Australia. Mandurah, Western Australia. MEWBURN,
> Robert W. http://www.billiongraves.com.

Increasingly, photographs of monumental inscriptions are being published online, typically as a free service.

> Monumental inscriptions. Canada. Edmonton, Alberta. MEWBURN, Frank
> Hastings Hamilton. http://www.findagrave.com.

Findagrave.com is another substantial resource with material from many parts of the world. It is created by volunteers so the data is not always accurate.

In most graveyards and cemeteries there will also be records of actual burials that have taken place and of where people have been laid to rest – a lair plan or a map of the plots. These can carry additional family information that is worth checking. They can be cited as regular documentary sources.

Referencing newspaper announcements and obituaries

Newspapers typically have a section devoted to formal announcements relating to personal events. These are the 'hatch, match and dispatch' entries for births, engagements/marriages, and deaths/burials. We treat these rather like vital records and we also think of the information as being primary since it was current at the time of writing.

The format for these is a little different from other nominal records and by convention is largely based on the Harvard style for newspaper articles – but has been given a few tweaks for genealogical use.

Elements in the reference are:

- Source type. [e.g., Marriage announcements, Death announcements, Obituaries, etc.]
- Country. [the country in which the newspaper is printed]
- Year of publication.
- *Name of newspaper.* [in *italics*]
- Day and month of publication.
- NAME, given name(s). [of person(s) referred to]
- Page number(s) and column code(s).
- Collection: Name of collection. [if the item was found within a database with multiple collections, then give the name of the collection]
- URL. [if the item was found online. See the URL guidelines for details]

Notes on elements
Typically, a key feature is the absence of an author for these entries so we use generic categories or source types to indicate their genealogical significance.

EXAMPLES

Birth announcements. England. 1859. *London City Press*. 29 Jan. RICHARDSON. p. 4a. Collection: British Newspapers, 1710–1965. www. findmypast.co.uk.

Note that 'p. 4a' means page 4, first column from the left (as in a, b, c, d across the page). Births are often a genealogical disappointment in that no given name is included – the entry simply saying 'son' or 'daughter' – naming being postponed until baptism.

Marriage announcements. England. 1861. *Southern Times*. 16 Jul. WILLARD, Bruce and FLORENCE, Sally. p. 23c.

In this instance, the actual newspaper has been seen by the researcher, so no URL appears. Note that newspaper titles are often replicated in different places, hence the need for country – the *Southern Times* is also a well-known South African newspaper.

Obituaries. Scotland. 1956. *Glasgow Herald*. 23 Apr. BISSELL, William M. p. 4c.
http://news.google.com/newspapers?nid=GGgVawPscysC.

A wide range of newspapers from several countries can be found at Google News.

Death announcements. Australia. 1942. *The West Australian*. 31 Jan. WOOLAMS,
Emma. p. 1b. http://trove.nla.gov.au/newspaper/search?adv=y.

Trove is a valuable adjunct to the sketchy BMD indexes available for Australia.

Of course, obituaries may appear in places other than newspapers; undertakers'
websites, for instance. An interesting example that acts as a substitute for a service
record for the Mounties – the Royal Canadian Mounted Police – appears in
their magazine the *RCMP Quarterly*. These obituaries have been indexed by the
Saskatchewan Genealogical Society. For example:

Obituaries index. Canada. Jan 1967. *RCMP Quarterly*. 32(3). CARTER, Leslie
James. http://saskgenealogy.com/databases/RCMP/RCMP_2008.htm.

The source type has been qualified by 'index' as this is a reference to where the
obituary can be found. In this case, the actual obituary has not been seen.

Referencing grants of arms

Armigerous ancestors provide rich opportunities for the genealogist as there may be
well documented histories for the family, while the arms themselves provide clues
to origins. Most of the material you will use to track down arms will, however, be
secondary in nature. The original grant, though, is a primary source. Whether such
a thing can be found, especially for more ancient examples, may be a challenge, but
authorities exist in many countries where records may be kept.

Scotland is exceptional in this regard in providing legal protection over the use of
arms and in enforcing it through the Court of the Lord Lyon. Records can be found
in the *Public Register of All Arms and Bearings in Scotland*.

The grants are a bit like official reports and can be treated similarly. They may well
include details of the application asking for a grant, and may provide genealogical
background in support of the claim.

Elements in the reference are:

- Author. [the granting authority]
- Country.
- Date. [when grant made]
- NAME, given name(s). [of grantee]

- Register title or Archival collection name. [The archival collection name only needs to be given if found at an archive where the material is placed in a named collection]
- Reference code/number(s). [if applicable and available. This refers to any useful codes or numbers referring to that source, collection and/or repository]
- Collection: Name of collection. [if the item was found within a database with multiple collections, then give the name of the collection here]
- URL. [if the item was found online. See the URL guidelines for details]

EXAMPLES

Court of the Lord Lyon. Scotland. 1672. MCDONALD, Lord. In: *Public Register of All Arms and Bearings in Scotland*. Ref. Coats of arms Volume 1 Page No. 102Z. Collection: Legal records: Coats of arms. www.scotlandspeople.gov.uk.

Older entries may not be informative. This simply lists the name, Lord McDonald.

Court of the Lord Lyon. Scotland. 1878. William Rae MACDONALD. In: *Public Register of All Arms and Bearings in Scotland*. Ref. Coats of arms Volume 10 PageNo 040Z. Collection: Legal records: Coats of arms. www. scotlandspeople.gov.uk.

In this case, the entry is beautifully illustrated and a full description of the claim is given with a blazon. It includes a description of the applicant's ancestry. The fact that he was Carrick Pursuivant in the Lyon Court may be a clue as to why it is such a nice entry.

In a similar manner, the College of Arms in London maintains a register with copies of the letters patent it has issued (covering England, Wales, Northern Ireland, Australia, New Zealand and some other Commonwealth countries). The Earl Marshal and the Kings of Arms Act under Crown authority when issuing arms but do not have the same powers of enforcement as in Scotland. The register is not available online, or publicly.

Many coats of arms have, however, been published. A readily available authoritative source is:

Fox-Davies, A.C. 1929. *Armorial Families: a directory of gentlemen of coat-armour.* 7th ed. London: Hurst & Blackett Ltd (which can also be found online at https://archive.org/details/armorialfamilies02foxd).

Of course, you may be fortunate and come across the original letters patent. These become the property of the grantee so they can be cited, in the fashion of any other original documents, if they have been seen by you.

Material records

The second of our major categories of record is to do with things, and with people's links to these things. We call them material. From a genealogy and family history perspective this category generally relates to property of every kind and the identification of people's relationships to it through ownership, occupancy, leasing, lending, licensing and so on. The property can be intellectual as well as physical, though the records we can readily get access to are mostly for the physical. For convenience, the discussion on these has been organised under three headings:

- Land and buildings;
- Personal possessions;
- Intellectual property.

Land and buildings

Records of ownership, tenancy and occupation, of land, and of property on that land, or minerals below it, can tell a lot about genealogy through paths of inheritance, and about family and social history by illustrating associations among people in an area.

These records can differ markedly between countries. Concepts of ownership and inheritance vary greatly and the legal systems within which they are settled vary at least as much. This chapter focuses on records from the British Isles.

None of this affects our principles of referencing. Where things differ, it will usually be in terms of the jargon used and the detail that needs to be provided to enable someone to home in on the exact record. Once again it can be helpful to use the idea of source types for categories of records within a particular system.

In England, the manorial system of the feudal Normans flourished up until the eighteenth century. No one other than the monarch owned land, at least notionally, and those whose rights were conferred directly by the monarch were still no more than 'tenants in chief'. Where they have survived, manorial records can provide a great deal of information illustrative of life in those communities. The National Archives carries some of these records while others appear in local archives. The *Manorial Documents Register* at TNA provides an index to the records for England and Wales and can be found at http://discovery.nationalarchives.gov.uk/manor-search.

Scotland, of course, has a separate legal system. Land-holding in Scotland operated under its own form of the feudal system which did not finally disappear until 2004.

It was a system with ancient origins that operated under ancient terms that not even the Scots are very familiar with, hence sasine, retours, and services of heirs.

We will touch briefly, too, on land records in Ireland.

Let's start with **English** records.

Referencing tithe maps and apportionments

In England, from the nineteenth century, highly detailed tithe maps were created showing every owned plot in each parish. These were associated with registers showing how plots were apportioned among owners and occupiers.

Elements in the reference are:

- Source type. [Tithe maps or Tithe apportionments]
- Country.
- Parish and county.
- Date.
- Owner/Occupier. [the name of whichever person is relevant for your referencing purposes. If both, then state which is owner and which is occupier]
- Plan number. [the number given to the plot as it appears on the map or in the apportionment]
- Image identifier. [for the scanned images, in the form Piece/Sub-piece/Sub-image]
- Reference. [the cataloguing reference]
- Place of publication: Name of publisher. [e.g. Kew, London: The National Archives]
- URL. [if the item was found online. See the URL guidelines for details]

EXAMPLES

Tithe maps. England. Egglescliffe, Durham. 02 Feb 1838. MEWBURN, John. Plan number: 92a. Piece 11; sub-piece 86; sub-image 001. Ref. IR 29/11/86. Kew, London: The National Archives. www.thegenealogist.co.uk.

A typical reference for an English tithea map, available online through a subscription service.

Tithe apportionments. England. Egglescliffe, Durham. 02 Feb 1838. MEWBURN, John. Plan number: 92a. Piece 11; sub-piece 86; sub-image 011. Ref. IR 29/11/86. Kew, London: The National Archives. www.thegenealogist.co.uk.

Note that the sub-image number is the only real difference in detail between the map and the apportionment.

Referencing manorial records

Manorial records have not all survived. For example, there is little for the Cleveland area of North Yorkshire. There is an official index contained within the *Manorial Documents Register* available online at the website of The National Archives. That lists 'court rolls, surveys, maps, terriers, documents and books of every description relating to the boundaries, franchises, wastes, customs or courts of a manor', but does not include title deeds.

Elements in the reference are:

- Source type. [manorial records]
- Country. [England]
- Place, county. [to the extent available]
- Date. [of document]
- Description of record. [the description used for cataloguing by the archive]
- Collection: Name of collection. [if the item was found within a database with multiple collections, then give the name of the collection]
- Reference. [cataloguing reference code used by the archive]
- Place: Name. [the place and name of the archive]

EXAMPLES ───

Manorial records. England. Brockdish Hall with Brockdish Earls Manor, Norfolk. 1818–1833. Minute book. Records of the Manors of Alburgh Rectory, Buxton with Members, Little Dunham, Gunshaws in Starston with Needham, Redenhall Hawkers, Holbrook and Coldham, Topcroft cum Denton, Brampton with the members and Other Papers. MC 1801/34, 829X1. Norwich: Norfolk Record Office.

This is one of two sets of minutes plus some rentals in a collection held at Norwich. The description does go on a bit, but that is how it is catalogued – go with it.

Manorial records. England. Manor of Burgh. 1685. Admittance at court leet. Collection: Deeds deposited by Yelloly and Burnett, Carlisle. DYB/1/74. Carlisle: Cumbria Archive Service.

This does not show up explicitly in the Manorial Documents Register so local archives do have to be checked for occasional extras.

Manorial records. England. Haddenham Manor, Buckinghamshire. 1712– 1743. Minute book, with other manors. Edinburgh: National Trust for Scotland.

This simply shows that manorial records may be held in unexpected places.

Manorial records. England. Romanby Manor, North Yorkshire. 1448–1450. Estreat roll (Allerton Liberty). SC 2/211/92. Kew, London: The National Archives.

And some are actually at The National Archives.

Referencing inquisitions post mortem

These are late-medieval documents and are somewhat specialised since they deal just with folk in the upper echelons of society who held lands of the Crown, so were tenants in chief. When they died, their lands reverted to the king if there was no heir, otherwise an inquisition (an inquest) was held, headed by an escheator and with a jury of local men to decide the heir and confirm the land holdings. An IPM can provide quite a lot of information about family members. It also names the members of the jury so identifies ordinary people from the area, and may help demonstrate the early presence of a family.

There is a published *Calendar of Inquisitions Post Mortem* at TNA. Early IPMs are in Latin. Many volumes have been digitised and can be found online at such sites as:

- British History Online, http://www.british-history.ac.uk/search/series/inquis-post-mortem,
- and Internet Archive at archive.org.

Elements in the reference are:

- Source type. [inquisitions post mortem]
- Country. [England]
- Place. [parish and county if available]
- Date. [of inquisition]
- NAME, given name(s). [name of the deceased person]
- Collection: Name of collection. [if the item was found within a collection]
- Archival reference code.
- Place: Name. [of archive]
- URL. [if the item was found online. See the URL guidelines for details]

EXAMPLES

Inquisitions post mortem. England. Worcestershire, Wiltshire, Hampshire. 1295. STURMY, Henry alias Le Estormi, de Stormy, Esturmy. Collection: Chancery: Inquisitions Post Mortem Series 1, Edward 1. Reference: C 133/71/21. Kew, London: The National Archives.

This example references an IPM held at The National Archives.

Inquisitions post mortem. England. Gloucester. 10 July, 10 Edward III. Margaret, late the wife of Fulk le FITZ WARYN. In: Sharp, J. E. E. S., E. G. Atkinson and J. J. O'Reilly, 'Inquisitions Post Mortem, Edward III, File 47', in *Calendar of Inquisitions Post Mortem: Volume 8, Edward III* (London, 1913). pp. 14–25. British History Online. http://www.british-history.ac.uk/inquis-post-mortem/vol8/pp14-25.

This example references a calendar entry in the digitised calendars at British History Online and embeds their preferred identification. Note the use of the regnal year.

Now let's look at **Scottish** records:

Referencing sasines

Our early Scottish ancestors weren't much into buying and selling land. You seized land by force of arms and defended it for as long as you could. As things became more civilised the language lingered on, so a sasine (pronounced *sayzin*) that records a change of ownership is for the 'seizing' of that land by its new owner – though now in a peaceful and purely administrative way.

Originally (before 1617) the fact of sasine would be witnessed by a notary public and recorded in their protocol book. Later, various Registers of Sasines attempted to capture all changes of ownership and continued to do so until 1981 when they were replaced by a new system of Registration of Title.

Elements in the reference are:

- Source type. [sasines]
- Country.
- Date of sasine.
- NAME, given name(s). [name of the principal in the transaction; more than one can be given]
- Reference code(s). [if applicable. This refers to any archival codes referring to that source, collection and/or repository]
- Repository name, [if applicable] Repository location. [if applicable]
- Collection: Name of collection. [if the item was found within an archival collection or a database with multiple collections, then give the name of the collection]
- URL. [if the item was found online. See the URL guidelines for details]

EXAMPLE ————————————————————————————

Sasines. Scotland. 02 Aug 1755. GRAY, Margaret. Particular register of sasines for the shires of Argyll, Dumbarton, Arran, Bute and Tarbert: second series.

(2 Aug 1755–20 May 1766) RS10/9/2. Edinburgh, Scotland: National Records of Scotland.

An example of a record examined at the archives.

Referencing retours

A retour is just a return. In other words, a notification sent in to the authorities (Royal Chancery) to indicate a change of ownership. The retour was the result of a local jury's deliberations on who was the rightful heir when someone died (a vassal under the feudal laws). There are further complexities, but this is not the place for them (see Bruce Durie's book if you want to find further detail).[17] The whole business of sorting this out was termed services of heirs so published versions are known as retours of services of heirs.

Elements in the reference are:

- Source type. [retours]
- Country.
- Date. [of retour]
- NAME, given name(s). [name of the inheritor]
- Reference code(s). [if applicable. This refers to any archival codes referring to that source, collection and/or repository]
- Repository name, [if applicable] Repository location. [if applicable]
- Collection: Name of collection. [if the item was found within an archival collection or a database with multiple collections, then give the name of the collection]
- URL. [if the item was found online. See the URL guidelines for details]

For retour information that has come from printed sources such as an index of services of heirs, use this referencing style:

- Source type. [retours]
- Country.
- Date. [of retour]
- NAME, given name(s). [name of the inheritor]
- In: Author. [of the printed source]
- *Title of the printed source.* [in *italics*]
- Vol. [volume number, if there is one]
- Entry: entry number. [if there is one]
- Place of publication: Name of publisher. [if applicable]
- Collection: Name of collection. [if the item was found within a database with multiple collections, then give the name of the collection]
- URL. [if the item was found online. See the URL guidelines for details]

Retours. Scotland. 02 Jul 1746. LUMSDEN, James. *Register of Acts and Decreets, 2nd Series, Durie's Office, 1st Series*. (04 Jun 1746–31 Jul 1746) CS22/423. Edinburgh: National Records of Scotland.

This retour was found within a register of acts and decreets and the register itself is held at the NRS in Edinburgh. Much of the information in the reference comes from the NRS's catalogue entry.

Retours. Scotland. 05 Oct 1666. LOVES, Agnes and Margaret. In: Thomson, Thomas. *Retours of Services of Heirs. Inquisitionum Retornatarum Abbreviatio 1544-1699*.Vol. III. Entry: 300. [CD-ROM] Edinburgh: Scottish Genealogy Society.

This special retour entry is from volume III of the published index and is entry 300.

Referencing Scottish royal charters

And then there are royal charters, basically recording gifts of property made by the Crown and appearing in two registers: the Great Seal and the Privy Seal, known by their Latin abbreviations as Reg. Mag. Sig and Reg. Sec. Sig. respectively.

Elements in the reference are:

- Source type. [Royal charters]
- Country. [Scotland]
- Place.
- Date. [of charter]
- NAME, given name(s). [of the recipient; name will be latinised]
- Regnal identifier.
- Entry number.
- Page.
- In: Editor, Publication *title*. Place: Publisher name.
- URL. [if the item was found online. See the URL guidelines for details]

Royal charters. Scotland. Edinburgh. 08 Jun 1624. GARDYN, Andree. 57 Jac. VI. No. 628, p. 218. In: Thomson, John Maitland, ed. 1894. *Registrum magni sigilli regum Scotorum: The Register of the Great Seal of Scotland*. Vol. 8. A.D. 1620–1633. Edinburgh: H.M. General Register House. https://archive.org/details/registrummagnisi08scot.

Archive.org has digitised copies of volumes from the register. Note that the entries in the register are in Latin.

Royal charters. Scotland. Strivelin. 30 Aug 1507. EDMONSTOUN, William. 20 Jac. IV. No. 1527, p. 219. In: Livingstone, M., ed. 1908. *Registrum secreti sigilli regum Scotorum: The Register of the Privy Seal of Scotland.* Vol. 1. A.D. 1488–1529. Edinburgh: H.M. General Register House. https://archive.org/details/registrumsecret00scotgoog.

In this case, the entries in the register are in Scots. Note: Strivelin is an ancient term for Stirling.

Referencing valuation rolls

There is nothing that an administration likes more than extracting tax from the population, and property taxes are a popular way to do that. To succeed in gathering the money, first you need to know what properties there are and who owns and occupies them. Scottish valuation rolls do that job and can be valuable to the genealogist in helping pin down those in the population deemed responsible enough to have a property. They resemble somewhat the tithe apportionments dealt with earlier.

Elements in the reference are:

- Source type. [valuation rolls]
- Country.
- Place. [parish and county]
- Date. [of valuation]
- NAME, given name(s), [the name of whichever person is relevant for your referencing purposes] status(es) [their role as proprietor, tenant or occupier]
- Reference. [the National Records of Scotland code]
- URL. [if the item was found online. See the URL guidelines for details]

EXAMPLES ───────────────────────────────────────

Valuation rolls. Scotland. Alford, Aberdeenshire. 1885. HAY, William, tenant. VR008700079. www.scotlandspeople.gov.uk.

A digitised image of the record is provided and may include more information about the property and the person's occupation. Note that the reference code covers four entries, for two of which William is tenant and two where he is proprietor.

An important thing to note about Scottish valuation rolls (and indeed other records that name people such as electoral listings) is that they tell us where people were at specific times. We can use them, therefore, as census substitutes. Notably, they can be used to trace people into more recent times beyond the census release dates. Clearly, we do not get family details but we may be finding the head of the household. At the time of publication, Scottish valuation rolls are available from 1855 up to 1935 – beyond any available census records.

Finally, we have **Irish** records.

Referencing Griffith's valuations

In Ireland, a form of valuation roll was created during the middle part of the nineteenth century, again to form the basis for taxation. This was created by Sir Richard Griffith for private holdings of property and land, and it related to ownership between 1848 and 1864. We get owners and occupiers noted so they serve as a census substitute.

From 1823 to 1838 there are also tithe applotment books. They provide just a name associated with a place so are of modest value to the genealogist though can offer confirmation of someone's link to a place.

Elements in the reference are:

- Source type. [Valuation rolls]
- Country.
- Place. [Townland, parish and county]
- Date. [of valuation]
- NAME, given name(s), [the name of whichever person is relevant for your referencing purposes] status(es) [their role such as lessor or occupier]
- Page. [page number(s)]

EXAMPLE

Valuation rolls. Ireland. Newtown, Agha, County Carlow. 1853. CUMMINS, John, occupier and BRUEN, Henry, lessor. p. 182. Collection: Ireland, Griffith's Valuation, 1847–1864. www.ancestry.com.

Newtown is the townland, particularly important in tracing people in Ireland, while Agha is the civil parish, again essential if trying to link to other record sources. Both occupier and lessor are identified for completeness.

Personal possessions

This is another area where not many records turn up that link things to people. A register of cars and who has owned them would fall into this category, but those are not commonly available.

Possessions also turn up when the authorities feel they can be used as a basis for taxation. Since tax is the primary impetus for such record keeping, examples of these are dealt with in Chapter 11.

An example where records can be found is where companies keep track of shareholdings and the shareholders. The shareholders are not always people, of course – nominee accounts may be used to disguise ownership. However, where people are identified there may also be evidence of individual transactions associated with them, including disposals under the terms of a will – so clues as to death and testamentary provisions may be found.

There may not be any relevant source types for possessions, so we use generic referencing principles.

EXAMPLE

GWR Shareholders. Registration of Probates and other documents, Vol 80, folio 101. 10 Sep 1900. MEWBURN, William. Collection: Great Western Railway shareholders 1835–1932 Image. http://search.findmypast.com/record?id=gbor%2fgwr%2f00198875.

In this case, there are transactions for the distribution, after death, of holdings in the Great Western Railway.

On a less savoury note, people can be treated as possessions. Records of slave holdings can be found in American censuses.

EXAMPLE

Census returns. 1850. United States. Greene, North Carolina. MEWBORN, Parrott. Collection: 1850 U.S. Federal Census – Slave Schedules. www.ancestry.com.

This is a schedule of slave inhabitants associated with a federal census. Sixteen enslaved people are identified but none are named. Only the owner is allowed a name.

There are also records for transported criminals sold into indentured employment, so again treated as possessions. Before Australia became available many thousands were shipped to British colonies in America. These people receive less attention than their Australian counterparts, presumably because today's Americans prefer to dwell on the more heroic exploits of the Jamestown settlers and those from the *Mayflower*. However, they are documented in valuable works by Peter Coldham:

Coldham, Peter Wilson. 1988. *The Complete Book of Emigrants in Bondage, 1614–1775*. Baltimore, MD: Genealogical Publishing Co. Inc.

Coldham, Peter Wilson. 1997. *The King's Passengers to Maryland and Virginia*. Maryland, USA: Family Line Publications.

In the first you can find entries like the arrival of the *Trotman* from Bristol in December 1770 where, from Yorkshire, there were:

Moburn, George: sold to –Amos
Unthank, Daniel: sold to Aquila Price – recognizance f.28 – runaway

Records for transportation to Australia are often available online and can be cited using our usual conventions.

> Convict transportations. York, Yorkshire. 31 Jan 1853. MEWBURN, Robert. (Conviction 09 Apr 1850). Collection: Australian Convict Transportation Registers – Other Fleets & Ships, 1791–1868. http://search.ancestry.com.

The wheels of justice could grind slowly. Prisoners were held in prisons or prison hulks until transport became available. In Robert's case, he was in Portland prison for three years before being shipped to Western Australia on the *Pyrenees*. The conviction date is part of this record and has been added to the reference just for information.

Sometimes there are records available for other forms of property such as the registration of motor vehicles, as in this example from Oregon, USA.

> Motor vehicle registrations. USA. Portland, Oregon. Aug 1911. BOLLMAN, Clarence. No. 5503. Collection: Oregon, Motor Vehicle Registrations, 1911–1946. www.ancestry.com.

Sadly, the type of car is not listed, but the owner's address is given.

Intellectual property

There are occasional court cases over this but in most areas there is little by way of administrative records. There are no registers of copyright owners. There are commercial organisations that manage licensing rights on behalf of various forms of copyright holder but their records are not available to the public.

One form of intellectual property registration that can be discovered, however, is for patents. This is also an area rife with litigation so procedural records are worth seeking out too.

> Patents. USA. 7 Jun 1887. TANGYE, Edward. Metallic fuses. Collection: U.S. Patent and Trademark Office Patents, 1790–1909. www.ancestry.co.uk.

People turn up in sometimes unexpected places (though not so unexpected in the case of this English entrepreneur). Note that we can use a conventional format for this type of record.

11

Procedural records

People get caught up in our systems of law and administration and may be named within records of their various proceedings. The role these individuals play may not be central, and the records may be mainly about the process, but names appear and fix people in particular situations, at particular times, like flies in amber. A person's presence in these records adds to their history.

A growing range of records from this procedural category is becoming available from all sorts of institutions and enterprises. Examples are given here from law and business. The general principles of referencing apply here as elsewhere.

Referencing travel records

People are often identified on various forms of travel record. In principle, this can help with an understanding of their movements and business activities and, even more so, can identify a migration. These records are procedural since they are principally to do with emigration and immigration, and the loading of ships (knowing who was on board in case they should founder).

Systematic maintenance of travel records is a late-nineteenth-century phenomenon associated with mass migration. Local travel up and down coasts, or to and from Europe and the UK, is rarely recorded.

If you are looking for evidence of travel it is worth bearing in mind that a journey may have been made in several segments. Emigrants from Europe in the late nineteenth century often left from Hamburg, but many stopped off in the UK and later journeyed separately from UK ports to North America. Similarly, land-fall in Australia could be followed by a further journey round the coast; arrivals at Quebec commonly led to ferry trips up-river into Ontario. Each segment will have its own record and a different carrier. Not all will be available, and each can be in a different repository or collection.

Many of these records are ship's passenger lists, compiled by a busy purser, and often very sketchy – *Mrs Whitmore* might be all the information provided. The spelling of names can be among the worst of all records. Records created by immigration authorities are likely to be more authoritative than those on emigration.

Elements in the reference are:

- Source type. [Travel records]
- Country. [the country which issued the record]
- Date of creation or of the event. [typically, a date of arrival or leaving]

- NAME, given name(s). [of the traveller]
- Record title or type of event. [typically, the heading on the document]
- Archival collection name. [if applicable. This only needs to be given if found at an archive where the material is placed in a named collection]
- Reference code/number(s). [if applicable and available. This refers to any useful codes or numbers referring to that source, collection and/or repository]
- Repository name, [if applicable and available] Repository location. [if applicable and available]
- Collection: Name of collection. [if the item was found within a database with multiple collections, then give the name of the collection here]
- URL. [if the item was found online. See the URL guidelines for details]

EXAMPLES ──

Travel records. New Zealand. 21 Apr 1928. ARMSTRONG, J.D. Passenger list for *S.S. Tutanekai* departing Apia. Collection: New Zealand, Immigration Passenger Lists, 1855–1973. https://familysearch.org/pal:/MM9.3.1/ TH-266-12529-30336-41?cc=1609792&wc=M9WV-C66:n791307836.

A fairly typical ship's passenger list. No repository was readily identifiable so could not be included.

Travel records. England. 08 Apr 1906. ADDERLEY, Francis (birth year 1870). Passenger list for *Victorian* departing Liverpool for Saint John, New Brunswick, Canada. Board of Trade (Great Britain). Collection: Passenger Lists Leaving UK, 1890–1960. www.findmypast.co.uk.

In this case, the assumed birth year, calculated from the age of the passenger given in the list, is included to ease identification, as there was another Francis ADDERLEY on this voyage, birth year 1899.

Travel records. Australia. Oct 1868. AMBROSE, Jane. Passenger list for *Sir Robert Sale* arriving at Melbourne, Victoria, Australia from Plymouth. Public Record Office Victoria. Collection: Inward Overseas Passenger Lists (British Ports). Microfiche VPRS 7666, copy of VRPS 947. Public Record Office Victoria, North Melbourne, Victoria. www.ancestry.com.au.

This references the original source material. The collection title for the scanned material used by Ancestry is 'Victoria, Australia, Assisted and Unassisted Passenger Lists, 1839–1923'. That title is an acceptable alternative.

Travel records. Germany. 05 Jul 1888. FISCHER, Eva. Departure of *Suevia* from Hamburg for New York. Collection: Hamburg Passenger Lists, 1850–1934. www.ancestry.com.

The Hamburg passenger lists are a major resource for emigration from Europe to the USA and UK in the later nineteenth and early twentieth centuries.

> Travel records. USA. 21 Jul 1882. FISCHER, Eva. Arrival of *Suevia* at New York from Hamburg. Collection: New York Passenger Lists, 1820–1957. www.ancestry.com.

Sometimes records for both ends of the journey can be found. Eva travelled with three children and records for them can also be found for their arrival at the Castle Gardens immigration centre in New York.

> Travel records. Canada. 30 May 1832. MEWBURN, Mr. Arrival of *Chambly* at Montreal from Quebec. In: Swiggum, S. and M. Kholi eds. 2011. 'Ships Passenger Lists', *TheShipsList*, online databases. http://www.theshipslist.com/ships/passengerlists/1832/cmay30.htm.

The record of a river ferry providing the segment of a journey. Note: TheShipsList is a particularly fine resource.

Referencing court proceedings

Legal systems generate a great deal of procedural material of value to genealogists and family historians. Where people have fallen foul of the law we may discover them in court papers and may get additional information about where they lived, what they did, and about other people associated with them. Disputes over land or other inheritance can be particularly profitable since family relationships may have to be spelled out over several generations to substantiate a claim.

Elements in the reference are:

- Name of court.
- Case description. [the kind of proceedings, including the name of our person of interest]
- Date. [of creation, or of event]
- Archival collection name. [if applicable. This only needs to be given if found at an archive where the material is placed in a named collection]
- Reference code/number(s). [if applicable and available. This refers to any useful codes or numbers referring to that source, collection and/or repository]
- Repository name, [if applicable and available] Repository location. [if applicable and available]
- Collection: Name of collection. [if the item was found within a database with multiple collections, then give the name of the collection here]
- URL. [if the item was found online. See the URL guidelines for details]

EXAMPLES ───────────────────────────────────

Crown Office. Precognition against Mary GRAHAM for the crime of bigamy. 1872. AD14/72/146. Edinburgh: National Records of Scotland.

A precognition is created before a trial and contains statements of fact from witnesses. Background material to the case, if you like.

High Court of Justiciary. Trial papers relating to Elizabeth WILSON for the crime of bigamy at George Square, Edinburgh. 14 May 1851. JC26/1851/541. Edinburgh: National Records of Scotland.

And this provides material from the trial proper.

High Court, Edinburgh. Trial papers relating to David LINNING, Jean NEIL for the crime of bigamy. 16 Nov 1835. JC26/1835/590. Edinburgh: National Records of Scotland.

Another example but from a different court.

Court for Divorce & Matrimonial Causes, London. Divorce record for BRETT, William Leopold. 1884. Ref. J77/330/9919. Kew, London: The National Archives. Collection: England & Wales, Civil Divorce Records, 1858–1915. http://ancestry.co.uk.

The original record is held at The National Archives but is now also available online.

Court of Chancery, London. Master Brougham's Exhibits: MARSHALL v BECKWITH. 1733. Ref. C 111/216. Kew, London: The National Archives.

A holding at The National Archives. The catalogue entry names seven people (not including any Marshall) who achieved agreement over the debts of the deceased William Moon. Most were related through marriages.

Court of Chancery, London. Six Clerks Office: Pleadings 1714–1758: MARSHALL v BECKWITH. 1731. Ref. C 111/503/37. Kew, London: The National Archives.

Earlier details from the Marshall v Beckwith case. This time the catalogue entry names seventeen people (again not including any Marshall) many of whom were related. A genealogical bonanza.

Assizes, Northern and North-Eastern Circuits. Criminal Depositions and Case Papers. MEWBURN, James. 1750. Ref. ASSI 45/24/2/78-80A. Kew, London: The National Archives.

A great deal of material relates to local courts. It often deals with minor disputes and infractions, but adds to the history of those involved. This case, for minor theft, led to transportation to Australia – extraordinary by today's standards.

> Court of Chancery, London. Six Clerks Office: Pleadings 1758–1800: PRUDOM v MEWBURN b.r. 1785. Ref. C 12/599/15. Kew, London: The National Archives.

Here a will was challenged, with ownership of an estate at stake. To support their claims, all involved had to set out, in detail, their relationship to the deceased. In effect, the case incorporates a comprehensive genealogy.

Referencing admission registers

A great many records relate to peoples' involvement with institutions such as hospitals, asylums, prisons and workhouses. The records are created for procedural reasons but do relate to individuals entering and leaving the system so, to all intents and purposes, can be thought of as nominal records.

Elements in the reference are:

- Source type. [admission registers]
- Country.
- Place.
- Date. [of creation, or of event]
- NAME, given name(s). [of person in the case]
- Archival collection name. [if applicable. This only needs to be given if found at an archive where the material is placed in a named collection]
- Reference code/number(s). [if applicable and available. This refers to any useful codes or numbers referring to that source, collection and/or repository]
- Collection: Name of collection. [if the item was found within a database with multiple collections, then give the name of the collection here]
- URL. [if the item was found online. See the URL guidelines for details]

EXAMPLES ───────────────────────────────

> Admission registers. England. Medway Union, Kent. 30 Jan 1882. JOHNSON, Ann. Collection: Medway, Kent, England, Poor Law Union Records, 1836–1937. www.ancestry.com.

An admission to the poorhouse. Ann was 92 and infirm so presumably could no longer look after herself, and had no family willing or able to do so.

> Admission registers. England. Burntwood, Staffordshire. 06 Jan 1890. AUSTIN, Chas. No. 87452. Collection: UK, Lunacy Patients Admission Registers, 1846–1912, Piece 29: 1890. www.ancestry.co.uk.

An admission to an asylum at Burntwood – 87452 is the admission number. Details in the register show that Charles remained there until his death in 1896.

> Admission registers. Scotland. Fisherton, Ayrshire. 01 Feb 1893. ANDREWS, Lizzie B. No. 44311. Collection: UK, Lunacy Patients Admission Registers, Provincial Licensed Houses. 1846–1912. Piece 11: 1880 February–1900. www. ancestry.co.uk.

This Scottish record is essentially the same as the English one. Lizzie was discharged in August, apparently recovered.

Referencing prison registers

Once people are caught up in the penal system they tend to be well documented. Elements in the reference are:

- Source type. [prison registers]
- Country.
- Place.
- Date of event.
- NAME, given name(s). [of person incarcerated]
- Reference code/number(s). [if applicable and available. This refers to any useful codes or numbers referring to that source, collection and/or repository]
- Archival collection name. [if applicable. This only needs to be given if found at an archive where the material is placed in a named collection]
- Collection: Name of collection. [if the item was found within a database with multiple collections, then give the name of the collection here]
- URL. [if the item was found online. See the URL guidelines for details]

EXAMPLES

> Prison registers. England. Chesterton, Cambridgeshire. 19 Mar 1868. BACKLER, Arthur. HO140. Calendar of Prisoners Tried at Assizes & Quarter Sessions – Chesterton Gaol. Collection: England & Wales. Crime, Prisons & Punishment, 1770–1935. http://www.findmypast.co.uk.

HO140 is the archival reference (HO being Home Office, the UK government department) while the Calendar is the original source document. The person named in this case is the felon; however, the victim is also named in the record and could be the person named in the reference if you were citing this to flesh out the history of that person.

> Prison registers. England & Wales. *Leviathan*, Portsmouth, Hampshire. 06 Oct 1818. BRADLEY, Thomas. Class HO9; piece 8. Collection: UK Prison Hulk Registers and Letter Books, 1802–1849. www.ancestry.com.

Hulks of ships moored offshore (the *Leviathan* in this case) were regarded as fairly secure places to shut prisoners away. They often served as way-stations prior to transportation.

Referencing poor relief records

The notion of poor relief developed over several centuries and did so differently in different legislations and under the direction of different pieces of legislation. The administration of poor relief could generate a significant body of records, particularly because of the need to determine responsibility, at a local level, for providing such relief. Whose purse stood to be depleted was often of more concern than the needs of the distressed individual, but that meant gathering significant information on the individual so that they could be allocated to the right 'beneficial' authorities.

Elements in the reference are:

- Source type. [poor relief records]
- Country.
- Place.
- Date of creation or of event.
- NAME, given name(s). [of person in the case]
- Archival collection name. [if applicable. This only needs to be given if found at an archive where the material is placed in a named collection]
- Reference code/number(s). [if applicable and available. This refers to any useful codes or numbers referring to that source, collection and/or repository]
- Collection: Name of collection. [if the item was found within a database with multiple collections, then give the name of the collection here]
- URL. [if the item was found online. See the URL guidelines for details]

EXAMPLES

Poor relief records. England. Potton, Bedfordshire. 21 Feb 1795. FULLER, James. Settlement examination. Ref. P64/13/4/27. http://bedsarchivescat. bedford.gov.uk/Details/archive/110198875.

A record held by the Bedfordshire Archives Service. This documents the gathering of evidence to determine whether Potton parish would be liable to provide relief. It states where James was born and also where he had been working.

Poor relief records. England. Potton, Bedfordshire. 21 Feb 1795. INSKIP, George. Removal orders from the parish. P64/13/2/81. http://bedsarchivescat. bedford.gov.uk/Details/archive/110198225.

Removal orders recorded movements from and into the parish resulting from the outcome of examinations to determine responsibility. These records are valuable indicators of a person's origin and subsequent movement.

Poor relief records. England. Bingley, Yorkshire. 1810. MIDDLETON, Susannah. Bastardy. Ref. 33D80/3/3. Collection: West Yorkshire, England, Bastardy Records, 1690–1914. www.ancestry.com.

This is a record of maintenance payments made by the father, Jonas Smith. The father's name could be included in the reference for greater clarity – or, indeed, he could be the subject of your investigation so his name could be the one in the reference.

Referencing taxation records

And then there are taxes. Not as inevitable as they say, depending on the skill of your accountant. Can't afford an accountant? Then, inevitable.

Governmental administrators have long been keen to know exactly who can be taxed. Lists have been compiled to show who was eligible for the privilege of paying by reason of having the use of a hearth, horse, pocket watch, piece of land, house, window, or whatever seemed like a good money-raising idea at the time. Often, however, there is little information in these lists beyond name and place but even that can position people in the past.

We generally construct references in relation to the kind of tax involved. The Hearth Tax records compiled for Charles II in the seventeenth century are a good start point – particularly for people with slightly unusual names. These records have been published online by the Centre for Hearth Tax Research at Roehampton University in London.[18]

A fine collection of diverse tax records from Scotland can be found on the ScotlandsPlaces website (www.scotlandsplaces.gov.uk). It offers free access to:

- Carriage Tax, 1785–1798
- Cart Tax, 1785–1798
- Clock and Watch Tax, 1797–1798
- Consolidated Schedules of Assessed Taxes, 1798–1799
- Dog Tax, 1797–1798
- Farm Horse Tax, 1797–1798
- Female Servant Tax, 1785–1792
- Hearth Tax, 1691–1695
- Horse Tax, 1785–1798
- Inhabited House Tax, 1778–1798
- Land Tax, 1645–1831
- Male Servant Tax, 1777–1798
- Poll Tax, 1694–1698
- Shop Tax, 1785–1789
- Window Tax, 1748–1798

English Land Tax records for various places can also be found online, as can Rates lists. More are being digitised from various jurisdictions so, for the genealogist, it is largely a matter of keeping on checking.

Elements in the reference are:

- Name of tax.
- Country.
- Date. [year when the tax was applied]
- Place. [Parish, County]
- NAME, given name(s). [of eligible person]
- Archival collection name. [if applicable. This refers particularly to an archival collection and usually needs to be given only if found at an archive]
- Reference code/number(s). [if applicable and available. This refers to any useful codes or numbers referring to that source, collection and/or repository]
- Collection: Name of collection. [if the item was found within a database with multiple collections, then give the name of the collection here]
- URL. [if the item was found online. See the URL guidelines for details]

EXAMPLES

Hearth tax. England. 1666. Norton, Stockton South West, County Durham. ADAMSON, Richard. Surname Index. http://www.hearthtax.org.uk/communities/durham/durhamsurnames1666L.pdf.

The record is just a line in the table that makes up the list. Stockton South West is the ward where Adamson lived, with Norton being the actual place. The only other information in the record is that his status was 'paying'. In some other records the number of hearths is included.

Land tax. England. 1788. St Katharine by the Tower, City of London. MEWBURN, James [tenant]. MS 6010/51, London Metropolitan Archives. www.ancestry.com.

The record is an entry in a register. The only other information is that Mary Fowler is the proprietor and tax was assessed at £3 15s. The location, however, may point to some maritime connection.

Farm horse tax. Scotland. 1797–1798. Bourtie [Bourty], Aberdeenshire. STRACHAN, John. Vol. 01, p. 32. http://www.scotlandsplaces.gov.uk/digital-volumes/historical-tax-rolls/farm-horse-tax-rolls-1797-1798.

In the record, each person is recorded with his farm name (Lochend in this case) – invaluable for accurate identification. The number of horses and duty payable then appears against him, giving some notion of the scale of his farming operation. Note, Bourty is an old spelling used in the roll.

Note, too, that ScotlandsPlaces is a site rich in diverse materials.

12

Other primary records: guidelines

A great array of records exists that do not fit any of our major categories or generic source types. Their purpose was often to capture information relating to some administrative (used in a broad sense) event. They are of interest to us when they identify individuals involved in these events. They provide additional snapshots of moments in these person's lives and serve to further illuminate their histories.

The general principles of referencing apply to these non-standard items in just the same way they apply to other records types. Who, when, what and where remain the keys to structuring. The fundamental idea that a future reader should be able to find the source again remains as strong as before.

Elements in the reference are:

- Creator/Author. [if available]
- Country.
- Place.
- Title/Description of resource.
- Date. [of creation, or of event]
- NAME, given name(s). [of person of interest]
- Archival collection name. [if applicable. This only needs to be given if found at an archive where the material is placed in a named collection]
- Reference code/number(s). [if applicable and available. This refers to any useful codes or numbers referring to that source, collection and/or repository]
- Repository location: [if applicable and available] Repository name. [if applicable and available]
- Collection: Name of collection. [if the item was found within a database with multiple collections, then give the name of the collection here]
- URL. [if the item was found online. See the URL guidelines for details]

Notes on elements
If in doubt over how to create a reference for an archival or genealogical source, using the general principles and elements above should give enough detail on your source.

If there is repository information available, it is helpful to give the repository's reference code, location and name, as these will help your reader find the resource again.

It is fine to add more information than suggested above, if there is any that might help towards unique identification.

EXAMPLES

> Commonwealth War Graves Commission. Wales. Holt (St Chad), Denbighshire. Casualty details. Death: 01 May 1918. CHATHAM, John Benmont. Royal Welsh Fusiliers. Service no: 60999. http://www.cwgc.org/.

The CWGC website is one of the great resources. This reference captures the soldier's regiment and service number as these can be invaluable when seeking out other types of service record. It also names his parents.

> McDonalds Ltd. Scotland. Glasgow. 16 Nov 1956. Attendance book entry showing James BURGOYNE present at general meeting of shareholders. House of Fraser Archive: Attendance books. Ref: FRAS 95. Glasgow, Scotland: University of Glasgow Archives.

McDonalds Ltd was the company holding the shareholders' meeting, thus is down as the creator of the source or the body responsible. The date is that of the meeting.

> London and North Western Railway. England. Liverpool. Dec 1852. COATES, A.W. Collection: UK, Railway Employment Records, 1833–1956. www.ancestry.co.uk.

Business records are increasingly becoming available. To a great extent, people are listed simply for the purposes of accurate accounting, and the information may consist of no more than a name. Nevertheless, particularly if some other way of associating a person with the business is available, the information can be useful.

> Anson, George E. England. 1849. *Privy Purse Ledger, Jun 1837–Dec 1849.* 17 Feb 1851. THOMPSON, D. RA/PPTO/PP/QV/QVACC.LED:1847. p. 305. Windsor: The Royal Archives.

There are many specialised archives sometimes holding unusual materials. The principles of referencing remain the same. This reference is to what is essentially a set of accounts. It could start just with Royal Archives as 'author' or, as here, you could use the name of the Keeper of the Royal Archives at the relevant time. He would not have written the entries in the Ledger, but did have responsibility for it – rather like a chief accountant or finance director. This style of reference confirms that the material is from his era.

> Goldsmiths' Company. England. London. *Apprenticeship and Freedom Index, 1578.* 'The Black Book'. London: Goldsmiths' Library.

The Guilds often maintain records of their members and of the apprenticeship they went through, and hold these in their own private libraries.

Referencing newspaper articles

Articles in newspapers, either about people or mentioning people, are invaluable for building up a family history. Unlike the Announcements described earlier, they are less stylised and may have identified authors.

Articles may be either primary or secondary depending on context or timeliness. We may treat a first-hand account of an event appearing in a newspaper ('news' items) as primary material though, since it has been processed through a journalistic filter, an element of discretion must be applied. Other articles appearing perhaps as 'opinion' pieces are more properly treated as secondary material.

Elements in the reference are:

- Author(s). [if the article does not have an author listed, use the title of the newspaper]
- Year of publication.
- Title of article.
- *Title of newspaper.*
- Day and month.
- Page number(s) and column line(s).
- Collection: Name of collection. [if the item was found within a database with multiple collections, then give the name of the collection]
- URL. [if the item was found online. See the URL guidelines for details]

Notes on elements

The Harvard approach has a reference style for newspaper articles so we've used it here. However, it's not so useful for 'family news announcements' as these often don't include a title, author, etc.; these are dealt with separately.

Older, large-format newspapers can be awkward to navigate through. However, almost always the text is arranged in columns for ease of reading. We use this in the reference to add precision to the location of the material being quoted. Columns are identified simply by lettering them in alphabetic sequence – a, b, c – left to right across the page.

EXAMPLES

McCarthy, Nancy. 1958. Slap down for crooked financier. *Portland Oregonian.* 27 Nov. p. 16c.

'p. 16c' indicates that the article is on the sixteenth page of the newspaper, in the third column of newsprint across the page.

Dillon, Frances. 2000. Fishing the deep pond: genealogists reach out across the Atlantic. *Scotsman.* 16 Feb. p. 3a. http://archive.scotsman.com/.

Access may not always be straightforward. In its online form, this is a subscription service.

Levien, J. Mewburn. 1929. Two Distinguished Whitby Families. *Whitby Gazette*. 08 Nov 1929. p. 4b–c.

Sometimes you get lucky as a genealogist and find that someone has published a family history as an item of local colour.

Caledonian Mercury. 1800. American commerce. *Caledonian Mercury*. 4 Jan. p. 2c. Collection: 19th Century British Newspapers. http://www.gale.cengage.com/.

Another example from a major subscription service.

Referencing official reports

Official reports can also be treated in a way that is similar to monographs. We have a fairly generic author in terms of a responsible individual, generally the head of the issuing organisation, or a role within the organisation, or a group of responsible officials.

Elements in the reference are:

- Author. [person, role, authority]
- Date. [when report issued]
- *Title*. [of report; in *italics*]
- Place: Name of publisher.
- Archival collection name. [if applicable. This only needs to be given if found at an archive where the material is placed in a named collection]
- Reference code/number(s). [if applicable and available. This refers to any useful codes or numbers referring to that source, collection and/or repository]
- Collection: Name of collection. [if the item was found within a database with multiple collections, then give the name of the collection here]
- URL. [if the item was found online. See the URL guidelines for details]

EXAMPLES

Dundas, W.P. 1861. No. 2814: First detailed annual report of the Registrar General of Births, Deaths, and Marriages in Scotland. *Abstracts of 1855*. Edinburgh: Murray & Gibb. Collection: House of Commons, Command Papers; Reports of Commissioners. http://gateway.proquest.com/openurl?url_ver=Z39.88-2004&res_dat=xri:hcpp&rft_dat=xri:hcpp:fulltext:1861-037165.

W.P. Dundas has been put in the 'author' slot since he was the Registrar General and the report was issued under his sole authority. The fact that minions may have slaved to produce it makes no difference to the reference though we could equally have simply said Registrar General as the author. The URL in this case requires an institutional account, however Histpop could equally be used.

Registrar General. 1870. *Fifteenth annual report of the Registrar-General on the births, deaths and marriages registered in Scotland during the year 1869; and fifth annual report on vaccination.* Edinburgh: Murray & Gibb. Collection: Online Historical Population Reports. http://www.histpop.org/.

Here we have used Registrar General as author. The title page of the report does not identify an individual, only the generic Registrar General post. He (W. Pitt Dundas) does sign an introductory letter to the Secretary of State that is placed at the beginning of the report so it would be possible to give him as a named author.

Census Commissioners. 1843. *Report of the commissioners appointed to take the census of Ireland for the year 1841.* Dublin: Her Majesty's Stationery Office. http://www.histpop.org/.

The year is when the report was actually published though it relates to material gathered a little earlier, and Dublin was where it was actually produced though the Report was delivered to Parliament in London.

Referencing legislation

Aspects of family history are often influenced strongly by laws in place at the time. If you are writing a history then you may need to work with people and records coming from several jurisdictions and may occasionally need to cite the laws that constrained them. These may be at national, federal, local, state, province, territory, barony, or from whatever level or area has the power to enact laws. References need to be precise in specifying the applicability of any law cited.

Rather like official reports, they can have cumbersome titles and it may not be immediately obvious how they are published.

Elements in the reference are:

- Title. [of legislation]
- Country. [jurisdiction where the legislation applies]
- Date of enactment. [this may be a date in the regnal year for UK legislation]
- Place: Name of publisher. [if available]
- Archival collection name. [if applicable. This only needs to be given if found at an archive where the material is placed in a named collection]
- Reference code/number(s). [if applicable and available. This refers to any useful codes or numbers referring to that source, collection and/or repository]
- Repository name, [if applicable and available] Repository location. [if applicable and available]
- Collection: Name of collection. [if the item was found within a database with multiple collections, then give the name of the collection here]

- URL. [if the item was found online. See the URL guidelines for details]

Notes on elements

In the case of UK legislation, the code based on regnal date is in itself a sufficient identifier and can be the whole reference, e.g. 26 Geo. II. c. 33.

If the citation is to a particular quotation from the legislation then the reference should include the page number where that is found.

EXAMPLES

Offences Against the Person Act. England. 1861. Vict. 24 & 25. c.100. Section 57. Bigamy. http://www.legislation.gov.uk/ukpga/Vict/24-25/100/ section/57/enacted.

The full title of this Act is 'An Act to consolidate and amend the Statute Law of *England* and *Ireland* relating to Offences against the Person' and it is dated 6 August 1861. The shorter form given in this reference is how it is usually referred to and how it can be found in searches. Note also the inclusion of the regnal year, the usual thing on the Acts. The URL leads straight to a section of the Act dealing with bigamy, so that is presumably what was being discussed in the text.

Family Law (Scotland) Act 2006 (asp 2), s.3. Scotland. 2006. Schedule 3 – Repeals. http://www.legislation.gov.uk/asp/2006/2/section/3.

Laws can be amended regularly and s.3 refers to amendments within Schedule 3 – Repeals. The item in brackets (asp) stands for Act of the Scottish Parliament, and is always in lower case.

An Act to Restrain all persons from Marriage until their former wives and former husbands be dead. 1 Jac. 1. c.11. England. 1603. In: *Statutes of the Realm*. Vol.4. Part 2. 1819. London: Eyre & Sons. p. 1028. https://tannerritchie. com/shibboleth/memso/browser.php?ipid=204756.

Details of ancient repealed laws for the UK are often not found on the legislation website. In this case, a published version has been digitised and is available on the web. Access, however, is through a subscription service.

An Act for the Better Preventing of Clandestine Marriage. 26 Geo. 2. c. 33. England. 1753. http://statutes.org.uk/site/the-statutes/eighteenth-century/1753-26-geo-2-c-33-prevention-of-clandestine-marriages/.

This is often called the Marriage Act, 1753 or Hardwicke's Marriage Act after its introducer, Lord Hardwicke. The original Act is hard to find in digital form but a few individuals have posted transcripts.

Referencing ephemera

As a family historian, you may well turn up printed material or celebratory objects that point to some people or events relevant to your researches. These can include playbills, political and religious tracts, public posters, lovespoons, marriage pitchers, commemorative items and such like. Insofar as they carry information you can use, you may wish to cite them. The identity of their creator or publisher may not be obvious so a generic style of reference will have to suffice.

Elements in the reference are:

- Descriptive title for the piece.
- Country.
- Place.
- Date.
- Place: Name of publisher. [if available]
- Archival collection name. [if applicable. This only needs to be given if found at an archive where the material is placed in a named collection]
- Reference code/number(s). [if applicable and available. This refers to any useful codes or numbers referring to that source, collection and/or repository]
- Repository name, [if applicable and available] Repository location. [if applicable and available]
- Collection: Name of collection. [if the item was found within a database with multiple collections, then give the name of the collection here]
- URL. [if the item was found online. See the URL guidelines for details]

Notes on elements

You may find this material in a museum rather than an archive, but the museum can be substituted for an archive or repository.

EXAMPLES ————————————————————————————

Poster for a voyage to Canada of the ship Columbus. England. Whitby, Yorkshire. 1832. Whitby Museum, Yorkshire: Whitby Literary and Philosophical Society. In: Harrison, Michael. 2009. Hewgill Family History website. http:// hewgillfamilyhistory.blogspot.co.uk.

This goes further in referencing terms than is usual since it identifies both the repository where the item is held and an independent website carrying an image of it.

Playbill. England. Vauxhall Gardens, London. 08 Sep 1842. PAYNE, W.H. Museum no. S.3-1983. London: Victoria & Albert Museum. https://collections.vam. ac.uk/item/O74605/vauxhall-gardens-final-masquerade-poster-ws-johnson/.

This one has been cited because of the appearance on the bill of W.H. Payne (ballet master at Covent Garden).

Pamphlet. Scotland. Undated (after 1988). *Kinneff Old Church: a Brief History*.
Kinneff, Kincardineshire: The Kinneff Old Church Preservation Trust.

A typical item that informs and publicises an historic building. This could almost be described as a (small) monograph since its content is potentially enduring though it does not possess many pretentions to physical permanence.

Referencing a letter, conversation or private correspondence

Information is often given to you informally in formats that defy all publishing rules (the table napkin is not unusual). As a researcher, you are influenced by it (the information, not the napkin) so it is important to let your readers know. Referencing in this case is an acknowledgement of the nature and origin of such influences. It adds to the audit trail even though the reader may not be able to go back to the source. The purpose of citation in this case is to add a level of transparency to your discussion.

The 'sources' you are dealing with will often be primary, though not always. The reference will not make that distinction so it is up to you to provide clarification in your text and point out the significance and reliability of the information.

Elements in the reference are:

- Author.
- Year of correspondence.
- Type of correspondence and name of correspondent [if available], day and month. [if available]

EXAMPLES ───────────────────────────────────

Gibb, F. 2001. Letter to Bryan Gibb, 27 November.

This is a communication recorded by and cited by the researcher so we would expect Bryan Gibb to be the researcher.

Brown, Gordon. 2012. Conversation with Felix Sadler, 18 December.

And here Felix Sadler is the researcher receiving, and noting, information from Gordon Brown.

The basic principle, where you refer to a more informal personal communication, e.g. letter, e-mail, phone call or conversation, is to provide as much detail as possible and note the nature of the communication. There is a clear expectation that you will have provided all relevant information about the nature of the correspondence within your text, at the point where you cite it. Your reader cannot readily follow up on this kind of reference, so relies on you to be clear and explicit when you mention it.

The most notable feature of references for these personal communications is that they contain no 'Where'. Your readers cannot access them. At best, they can try to communicate with you to ask about them, if you are prepared to permit such dialogue.

13

Images

Images provide us with a fascinating can of worms. Here we are thinking of pictures of people, or occasions, or things that are of family history relevance. We are not concerned with scanned images of BMD records for instance. However, many media can be used to capture images. They may even be moving video, or in the form of three-dimensional holograms.

An image may be of the moment and regarded as a primary source, while a painting may have been made from a photograph and executed years later. Do we know who made the painting and when?

Interpretation is, therefore, a matter that requires great care. Photographs are often unidentified; clothing may be the best clue to the era in which it was taken. Even when names are written on the back we are unlikely to know who did that, or when, so a judgement on the reliability of such an inscription may not be easy.

Images of places are similarly tricky. The location may be uncertain, dating may be problematic and, indeed, the place may have been substantially altered, or, if it is a building, may no longer exist. Books have been published on how to extract evidence from images.[19]

Elements in the reference are:

- Source type. [images]
- Type of format. [e.g. photograph, lithograph, painting, film]
- Date. [if this is not known, an estimate should be made, e.g. *c.* 1880; *c.* 1900–1905]
- NAME, given name(s). [of person(s) appearing, if known and relevant]
- Principal subject. [e.g. wedding group; portrait; holiday snap etc.]
- Place taken, or made. [if known]
- Place found, or held.
- Image creator. [if known]
- Archival reference. [if relevant]

EXAMPLES ————————————————————————

Images. Photograph. 06 Mar 1870. James CAMPBELL and Ann BRYCE wedding group. Edinburgh. James Williamson, photographers. Private collection of George B. Campbell, Dundee.

Group photograph of wedding guests outside St George's Church, Charlotte Square, Edinburgh.

Images. Photograph. 2011. Memorial to Andrew and Ann FRASER at Fearn
Abbey. Roddie Macpherson, photographer. In: Ross & Cromarty Roots
website. http://gravestones.rosscromartyroots.co.uk/picture/number15125.
asp?st=Andrew%20Fraser.

Increasingly, large numbers of pictures of gravestones and other monuments are being
made available online.

Images. Photograph. 2013. Memorial of Mary of Burgundy (1457–1482).
Church of Our Lady, Bruges, Belgium. Ian Macdonald, photographer.
In: Register of Qualified Genealogists website. http://www.
qualifiedgenealogists.org/about.

Permission to use images from websites always needs to be sought.

Images. Video. 1986. Interview with Mrs. Mary Neilson on her 104th birthday.
Aberdeen, Scotland. 'North Tonight', BBC TV Scotland. Private collection
of Ian G. Macdonald.

Increasingly, items like this can be found on YouTube so a URL could be provided.

Images. Painting. 1877. William ALEXANDER. Illustration for *Johnny Gibb
of Gushetneuk*. Sir George Reid, painter. Museums No. ABDAG004061.
Aberdeen, Scotland: Aberdeen Art Gallery and Museums Collections.

This reference arises from a permission granted to use a scanned image of the painting.
However, that image is not publicly available to download so the actual painting is
referenced.

14

Maps

Maps are crucial to the better appreciation of family history and to the understanding of communities. Some, of course, identify the owners of properties and land, so can be invaluable to the genealogist.

It is not always easy to discover details of a map's creation so its location may be particularly important for referencing purposes.

Elements in the reference are:

- Map maker.
- Year of issue.
- Title of map.
- *Map series*, [in *italics* and if known. If there is a series it, like a journal, is treated as the publication] Sheet number, Scale.
- Place of publication: Publisher.
- Archival collection name. [if applicable. This only needs to be given if found at an archive where the material is placed in a named collection]
- Reference code/number(s). [if applicable and available. This refers to any useful codes or numbers referring to that source, collection and/or repository]
- Collection: Name of collection. [if the item was found within a database with multiple collections, then give the name of the collection]
- URL. [if the item was found online. See the URL guidelines for details]

EXAMPLES

Ordnance Survey. 1868. Forfar. *Ordnance Survey of Scotland One-inch to the mile maps of Scotland, 1856–1891*, sheet 57. Southampton: Ordnance Survey Office. http://maps.nls.uk/view/74490367.

This is an example of the first edition.

Ordnance Survey. 1860. Town plan of Hawick. *Ordnance Survey large scale Scottish town plans, 1847–1895*, sheet xxv.3.24, 1:500. [?]: Ordnance Survey. http://maps.nls.uk/townplans/hawick.html.

Maps can deal with small areas. Town plans, perhaps along with census returns, can be helpful to the genealogist – try plotting the location of all family members in the town!

Ordnance Survey. 2006. Chester and North Wales. *Landranger series*, sheet 106,
1:50000. Southampton: Ordnance Survey.

Ordnance Survey have been producing maps over a long period. These maps can
illustrate the history of an area when a series of issues provide a picture of the
developing landscape and its habitation.

Roy, William. 1747–55. Cabrach, Banffshire. *Military Survey of Scotland*.
Edinburgh: National Library of Scotland. http://maps.nls.uk/geo/
explore/#zoom=12&lat=57.3311&lon=-3.0642&layers=3.

A wonderful example of an early topographical map – in this case created in the wake
of the Jacobite uprising to assist in subduing the Highland clans.

Cruchley, G.F. 1842. *Cruchley's new Plan of London improved to 1842*. London:
G.F. Cruchley.

A fine fold-up map of London published from premises in Fleet Street. Editions
ranged from 1827 to 1846. Then, as now, many commercial maps were produced.

Another form of map that may be available is the tithe map (as discussed above in
Chapter 10). These are highly detailed, showing every plot in a parish and identifying
its owner and occupier. A wonderful resource for the genealogist and family historian.

15

Using the referencing principles in your own writing

As you have seen, we do not recommend the style sometimes found where a citation appears in parentheses (round brackets) embedded within the text and immediately after the clause being referred to. Using a numeric superscript citation and keeping the reference separate from the text improves readability by removing a visual distraction.

The citations point to where a reference can be found. We put them in either footnotes or endnotes.

Footnotes and endnotes

These terms are fairly self-evident. Footnotes appear at the foot of a page, generally in a ruled-off area and often in a smaller font. Endnotes appear at the end of a document. We recommend that they be formatted identically. References to sources are not inherently thrilling pieces of text, despite their enormous value, so there is a good case to be made for always consigning them to endnotes.

Footnotes that are not references are still visually distracting so should be used sparingly – only where an explanation of some term is needed, or where you have an overwhelming urge to digress into some interesting aside that is not immediately relevant to your text. In this book, all attempted footnotes have been wisely consigned by the publisher to a terminal notes section.

Using these notes

Link the quotes and data cited in your text to their references, in one of the notes areas, using the numeric system, i.e. with numbers in superscript that are placed after the material being cited or after the full stop of the sentence in which the quote/data appears, for example:

> The native Scots, who had been restrained only by fear of the king, now, as the army broke up in confusion, set about slaying all the English in their own ranks on whom they could lay hands, while those who were able to escape, we are told, took refuge in the royal castles.[1] Or, as the Scottish historian puts it, 'the Scots and Galwegians, when their king was captured, made constant attacks upon their French and English neighbours and slew them without mercy'.[2]

1   Frank, Cecilia. 1975. *A general history of Scottish warfare in the early modern era*.
     Oxford: Oxford University Press. p. 136.

2   McConnell, Duncan. 1865. *O fateful day: a bloody time in old Scotland*. Edinburgh:
     White Scribe Press. p. 865.

When a sentence provides several facts, e.g. a person's birth, marriage and death dates, each from a separate source, then place the appropriate superscript number for citation purposes within the sentence after the individual fact it refers to. Do not string them all together at the end of the sentence. It looks dreadful and it may not be obvious what each number relates to.

References to all sources directly quoted or used for data, and thus with associated superscript numbers, should appear in a footnote or endnote section. For genealogical/ archival sources, references should follow the guidelines provided in this book. For secondary sources, references should follow the 'Harvard' style, again as outlined here.

These days, the use of Latinisms is increasingly frowned on, because they act as a barrier to understanding for many readers and can seem pretentious. Writers commonly will choose not to use them. If, despite that, you are wedded to the older traditions, you can use the term *Ibid*. (an abbreviation for *Ibidem* meaning 'the same place' in Latin) to refer to the same author and source in an immediately preceding reference, along with the relevant page numbers. The term *op. cit*. (an abbreviation for *opus citatum* meaning 'the work cited' in Latin) can be used to refer to a reference previously cited (but not immediately preceding) by the same author and source.

1   Smith, James, ed. 1992. Scottish local government. Edinburgh: Edinburgh
     University Press. pp. 10-12.

2   Ibid. pp. 17-18.

3   Ibid. p. 36.

4   Williams, Arthur and George Goldstone. 2004. Poverty in 19th century Edinburgh.
     London: HarperCollins. p. 56.

5   Census returns. Scotland. Kingsbarns, Fife. 06 Jun 1841. ANDERSON, Alexander.
     441/00 001/00 007. http://www.scotlandspeople.gov.uk.

6   Williams, op. cit. p. 102.

The use of *op. cit*. is particularly annoying as it requires the reader either to have a good memory for earlier references or to search back to find them.

If you wish to eschew Latin to make your material accessible to all then simply provide the full reference each time. It is more polite to do that these days.

Bibliographies

If writing a book, then you may wish to include a bibliography (in addition to endnotes). This is a complete list of the sources you have made use of. Genealogical practice is to split this into separate sub-lists for primary and secondary sources.

Bibliographies are simple lists where each source appears once only and where there is no link back to where it is used in the main text. They provide an easy way for the reader to get an understanding of the range of materials used by the author. The references are arranged in alphabetical order by the author's surname, or item title if there is no author. As mentioned earlier, the definite article, 'the', is not used within these names to ensure a more natural alphabetic sequencing.

Primary sources in bibliographies

The bibliography lets the reader see, in summary, all the different sources referred to within the publication.

Heavy use of primary sources is a distinctive feature of genealogical work, which is why we list them separately. All the primary sources used and referred to in footnotes/endnotes, are listed in that section of the bibliography. However, we make use of a generic entry to indicate the source type. If you like, we treat the source type as if it were a book, so we might list 'Census returns. England. 1881.' as a referenced source. We may have cited separately many individual records from that census but we do not list each usage in the bibliography. For the sake of simplicity, we also give just the year rather than the full date. The bibliography will, therefore, carry an entry that shows:

Census returns. England. 1881. http://www.ancestry.co.uk.

Of course, because it was accessed online we still include the root web location.

This generalisation can be taken further in the census case, where broadly the same kind of reference is repeated for each ten-year interval. We can form a single bibliographic entry by indicating the range of years cited. For example:

Census returns. Scotland. 1841–1911. http://www.scotlandspeople.gov.uk.

If every available census has been used as a source, or:

Census returns. England. 1851–1891. http://www.ancestry.co.uk.

If censuses from only those years have been used.

Census returns. England. 1841–1939. http://www.findmypast.co.uk.

This includes the 1939 Register as a quasi-census. That applies to England and Wales only when dealing with online accessible material.

This style of abbreviation is eminently sensible. The reader can be expected to assume that if you looked at censuses you will have checked out all those that might have been relevant. If, instead, you give a list of each individual Federal, Scottish, English, Welsh census and so on, it will not be an aid to understanding – almost the opposite, it will bore your reader into a catatonic state.

Secondary sources in bibliographies

Secondary sources make up most of what appears in a traditional bibliography. They include such things as books, book chapters, journal articles, newspaper articles, theses and web resources that have been cited. They can also include sources that have been used, or consulted, during the investigation even when these have not been explicitly cited in the text. This part of the bibliography can, therefore, point the reader to other material that is relevant for broader study.

The focus, as with primary material, is on the source used rather than specific citations from that source. That means we do not include any mention of page numbers, as we might have done in the original reference. When we list journal articles or chapters within an edited book we still, though, have to be clear about the scope of these works within the larger publication. For that reason, page numbers for the boundaries of the work are included (the range that covers the whole work not the pages that were specifically cited previously). For example:

> McBrien, Angela. 2008. First boilings or the sticky history of sweets in Scotland. *History notes.* 4(13). pp. 43–75.

In this instance, the original citation mentioned just page 45, while 43–75 is the whole article.

EXAMPLE

Bibliography

Primary Sources

Baptisms index (PR). England. Collection: Births and Christenings, 1538–1975. https://familysearch.org.

Births (CR). Scotland. http://www.scotlandspeople.gov.uk.

Census returns. Scotland. 1841–1911. http://www.scotlandspeople.gov.uk.

Census returns. England. 1881. http://www.ancestry.co.uk.

Secondary Sources

McBrien, Angela. 2008. First boilings or the sticky history of sweets in Scotland. *History notes.* 4(13). pp. 43–75.

Rumpole, Edward. 1997. 'Managerial expert systems and organisational change'. In: Withers, R.J. and R.A. Patroch, eds. *Change management: a reader.* Chichester: Wiley. pp. 135–170.

Smith, James, ed. 1992. *Scottish local government.* Edinburgh: Edinburgh University Press.

Souvenir album of Annapolis and Digby, Nova Scotia. [n.d.] Annapolis, Nova Scotia: Atlee's Drug and Stationary Store. http://archive.org/details/cihm_64440.

Williams, Arthur and George Goldstone. 2004. *Poverty in 19th century Edinburgh.* London: HarperCollins.

16

Working with software

There are many software systems that can be useful to the genealogist and often they provide the ability to record references. Some enable you to create your own database of references, standing alone from other work; others enable you to create family trees and, as part of that process, to link references to people within the tree. These are bibliographic and genealogical software respectively.

Bibliographical referencing software

Bibliographical referencing software can assist you, particularly when creating references for your secondary sources. A good example is EndNote, but there are also free products such as Mendeley, a reference and PDF organiser, and Zotero, which support various versions of the Harvard style. Most bibliographic referencing software is configurable which means you can change the output style to match ours. You'll need to check the software's help section for configuration information.

These systems will automatically format your references in your selected, defined style. You can choose from a number of options. They also provide a good way of organising your references.

This type of software is not designed for use with genealogical and archival primary sources so it will require effort on your part to get it to work well.

Genealogical software

Genealogical software packages sometimes provide a facility to attach references to facts as you record them. That is a good thing to be able to do. However, make sure you set up the facility so that you can record the references using the styles given in this book.

Sometimes templates are provided for referencing. They are unlikely to match the advice offered in this book so your aim should be to tailor them to match the good practice outlined here.

Commonly, genealogical software packages display, or allow people to display, family trees on the web. Please do not cite other people's trees as a source. The fact that a family tree has been created within some sound genealogical software environment unfortunately does not provide assurance that it has been done well, or that entries in the tree created by the tree owner are sound. There is a lot of nonsense on the web so even when something looks like a good fit to your own research do not accept it until you can get back to real primary sources.

Composite trees are also emerging on the web. These are created by systems that trawl other trees and merge them to form an apparently more comprehensive tree. However, the garbage-in-garbage-out (GIGO) principle applies here. Linking one lot of poor data to another equally poor lot just creates an even less reliable combination. Composite trees need to be approached with a particularly long barge-pole.

Finding a Macdonald family tree on Ancestry or on Genes Reunited, or some other such environment, may provide insights that help you clarify the structure of your own tree but you should never cite that tree as such. If that tree provides good source references then check them out and, if they prove reliable, use those references (in our format) in your own work. Copying and pasting from other people's unverified trees is not to be recommended; potentially you are corrupting your own pristine work.

17

Future citation

'The Truth is Out There.'
(*The X-Files* tagline)

Well, truth can be a slippery concept and, like the TV series, genealogical investigations never really end since new sources of information are constantly being turned up, and also created. Nevertheless, we believe that the principles outlined in this book will be sufficiently robust to enable you to handle anything that comes along.

Life's audit trail

The so-called 'vital' records, BMD, give us the barest dimensions of a life. There are, however, other significant events commonly recorded, and a great many additional things, often seemingly insignificant at the time, that are recorded by others. These are

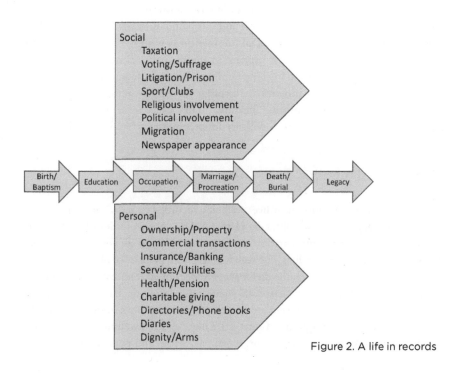

Figure 2. A life in records

all products of the remarkable set of processes that the present world deems necessary to administer our journey through life. Figure 2 illustrates some of these things, all of which can leave traces in records.

Given time, the researcher will wish to explore all these and more, and will need to cite the use of them. The principles outlined in this book should suffice for doing that.

An expanding world of administrative records

Today there is prodigious growth in the recording of information about individuals in our societies. Figure 2 just touches lightly on it. Given a modest time lag, much of the information now being recorded may be made accessible to researchers.

Consider supermarkets and online retailers. The data they gather on individual shoppers enables them to predict with great accuracy exactly what things they will buy, and when, and whether they will buy a new product, if offered. In principle, they can also track the economic fortunes (through types, quantities and cost of products purchased), and geographical movements, of every individual through their lifetime.

Systems of government are increasingly under attack, and one response is to gather increasingly detailed and diverse forms of information on members of the populace, their movements (car number plates are automatically scanned on major roads), their use of government services (health, social security, justice and so on) and their communications with one another. In time, too, some of that may become available (or be leaked). As we've seen, that information can extend to business dealings, and the more that business records become public the more we can extend our study of social behaviour into that field. Parish and village life is barely relevant to today's society where the greater part of social interaction is within a business or online context – and for many people that happens in a multi-national way.

The family historian needs to become familiar with a whole new range of records that follow the fortunes of individuals through the events, activities, enterprises and systems that define and outline their lives. They carry information that could illuminate family histories and they will, no doubt, eventually become available.

Mining social media?

On top of increased administration, lives are being recorded by individuals themselves, in detail, on every form of social media platform. They carry profiles of participants, the identity of associates, information about events engaged in, personal tastes and places visited, attitudes and beliefs. The web is awash with pictures of plates of food – in future you will be able to track the dietary preferences of your ancestors. Commonly, social media systems also use geographical positioning data to track the movements of people in their everyday lives (using it ostensibly to provide information about nearby things and services that might be of interest). They capture dwelling patterns, places used for work, exercise, entertainment, social gatherings and personal networking.

This information is already being used by police forces in criminal enquiries, and to investigate terrorist threats.

When you bring all the administrative, governmental, business and social media records together there is potential to map out a person's life in great detail. The events they have participated in, their interests, personal behaviours, preferences and proclivities are all there. This is either fascinating or terrifying, but certainly suggests that family historians, in future, may have the capacity to develop life stories in unimagined detail.

Citing social media

There is no inherent objection to Facebook entries being cited or Twitter conversations or LinkedIn statuses. YouTube, Snapchat and Instagram (and others yet to storm our joint consciousness) are being used to capture life events, so these too will be cited.

References to them should look pretty much like those used for other electronic communications. They need to identify who posted, when, on what system and on what subject. Since these are essentially broadcast (rather than narrowcast like letters and e-mails) there will be no recipient.

A word of warning, though. An important matter when citing any of these ephemeral outbursts is to determine the true originator. Material is endlessly copied and re-transmitted on social media – do you have the right person (and are you sure it's not 'fake news')?

Linking to DNA analyses?

DNA analyses provide hard personal data which may provide strong evidence for familial linkages. It makes perfect sense for this to be recorded in some way, and cited as evidence in proving identity.

At the lowest level, the complete set of strings of base-pairs identified in an analysis provide absolute identification for an individual. However, this is not the kind of information that is suited to referencing (or that you might want to make public). The base-pairs are like words in a book. It is the book for the person we need to cite.

The 'book', then, is the test result produced by the testing company for a customer. That means it is a specific instance of testing that we need to reference because the results from it tell us what all the mutations, SNPs, and such like, looked like when that test was done. Testing is not guaranteed to provide absolutely correct results and, of course, the science is constantly improving and, along with it, the testing regimes. Every different test that is done may give a somewhat different result and, each time, that latest result can be referenced.

Citing DNA analyses

For these results to be referenceable they need to be in a place where potentially anyone can go to see them. That is most likely to occur when test results have been uploaded to a website and made publicly available for comparison with other peoples' results.

If that has happened, and the DNA's owner is happy to be mentioned, then key elements making up a reference will be:

- DNA (type tested) test results. [type tested will be e.g. Y-chromosomal, Autosomal-chromosomal, Complete-chromosomal, Mitochondrial]
- Date. [test date]
- NAME, given name(s). [of the subject person]
- Kit number. [or vendor's equivalent term]
- Vendor.
- URL. [to where the item was found online. See the URL guidelines for details]
- Other elements can be added as required.

Be aware, though, that developments in gene technology, no doubt ostensibly to avoid undesirable genetically triggered medical conditions, will introduce difficulties for future genealogical investigators. The replacement of mitochondria in an ovum, as can now be done, introduces a complete break in the line of female succession when judged by mitochondrial DNA. Similarly, gene editing will lead to discrepancies between parental and child gene patterns. Without a clear and visible record of such procedures, mystifying discontinuities will emerge. However, the impact of this will not be felt by genealogists for some time yet.

18

Endpoint: or a new beginning

Thank you for braving the journey thus far.

This book sets out a simple approach to referencing sources and showing where they may be found. By doing that it should play an important role in raising standards in genealogical practice. That is its aim.

Whenever you make clear what evidence you are using to reach a genealogical conclusion, and state where it can be seen, you are lighting a candle for better, more credible, genealogy. If you pursue the principles outlined here you will be doing a service to genealogy and family history and setting a valuable example to researchers who follow.

Without good references, you add more garbage to the fetid pile that makes up so much of the ill-founded nonsense that befouls the web masquerading as family trees. Citing sources and providing references is a key to clarity and a way of illuminating findings and decisions.

All genealogical conclusions are based on an assessment of probabilities. There are no absolute facts since every record can contain errors. The best genealogy is therefore that which sets out the evidence gathered and describes how a conclusion was reached. More than that, and most importantly, it leaves an audit trail that allows others to find that evidence and check it for themselves. Assurance, or assurability, is the best way forward for our discipline. The principles outlined here will enable you to take the first step. Bon voyage!

Bibliography

Adams, Douglas. 1979. *The Hitchhiker's Guide to the Galaxy.* London: Pan.

American Psychological Association. 2009. *Publication Manual of the American Psychological Association,* 6th ed. Washington, DC: American Psychological Association.

Anglia Ruskin University Library. *Harvard system of referencing guide.* http://libweb. anglia.ac.uk/referencing/harvard.htm.

Board for Certification of Genealogists. 2014. *Genealogy Standards.* Nashville and New York, USA: Ancestry.com.

Carter, Paul and Kate Thompson. 2005. *Sources for Local Historians.* Chichester, West Sussex: Phillimore.

Centre for Hearth Tax Research. 2011. *Hearth Tax Online: Householders in late 17th century England.* http://www.hearthtax.org.uk.

Chicago Editorial Staff. 2010. *The Chicago Manual of Style: The Essential Guide for Writers, Editors and Publishers.* 16th ed. Chicago: University of Chicago Press.

Coldham, Peter Wilson. 1988. *The Complete Book of Emigrants in Bondage, 1614–1775.* Baltimore, MD: Genealogical Publishing Co. Inc.

Coldham, Peter Wilson. 1997. *The King's Passengers to Maryland and Virginia.* Maryland, USA: Family Line Publications.

Durie, Bruce. 2009. *Scottish Genealogy.* Stroud, Gloucestershire: The History Press.

Durie, Bruce. 2013. *Understanding Documents for Genealogy & Local History.* Stroud, Gloucestershire: The History Press.

Fox-Davies, A.C. 1929. *Armorial Families: a directory of gentlemen of coat-armour.* 7th ed. London: Hurst & Blackett Ltd.

Grenham, John. 2006. *Tracing your Irish Ancestors,* 3rd ed. Baltimore, MD: Genealogical Publishing Co., Inc.

Herber, Mark. 2004. *Ancestral Trails the Complete Guide to British Genealogy and Family History.* 2nd ed. Reprinted 2006. Baltimore, MD: Genealogical Publishing Co., Inc.

British History Online. 2017. *British History Online* website. London: Institute of Historical Research and School of Advanced Study, University of London. http://www.british-history.ac.uk.

Internet Archive. *Internet Archive* website. San Francisco, CA: Internet Archive. https://archive.org.

LearnHigher: Centre for Excellence in Teaching & Learning. *Referencing.* http://www.learnhigher.ac.uk/writing-for-university/referencing/.

Mantel, Hilary. 2017. Resurrection: The Art and Craft. *Reith Lectures*. BBC Radio 4. http://www.bbc.co.uk/programmes/b08vkm52.

Modern Language Association of America. 2016. *MLA Handbook*, 8th ed. New York: The Modern Language Association of America.

National Archives (Great Britain). *Manorial Documents Register*. http://discovery. nationalarchives.gov.uk/manor-search.

Historic Environment Scotland, National Records of Scotland, and National Library of Scotland. *ScotlandsPlaces* website. www.scotlandsplaces.gov.uk.

Library of Congress. *Library of Congress Names (NACO Authority File)* website. http:// id.loc.gov/authorities/names.html.

Shown Mills, Elizabeth. 1997. *Evidence! Citation & Analysis for the Family Historian*. Baltimore, MD: Genealogical Publishing Co., Inc.

Shown Mills, Elizabeth. 2009. *Evidence Explained: Citing History Sources from Artifacts to Cyberspace*. 2nd ed., revised 2012. Baltimore, MD: Genealogical Publishing Co., Inc.

Shrimpton, Jayne. 2014. *Tracing Your Ancestors Through Family Photographs: A Complete Guide for Family and Local Historians*. Barnsley, Yorkshire: Pen & Sword Family History.

Szucs, Loretto Dennis and Sandra Hargreaves Luebking, eds. 2006. *The Source: a Guidebook to American Genealogy*. 3rd ed. Provo, UT: Ancestry.

Wrigley, E.A., ed. 1973. *Identifying People in the Past*. London: Edward Arnold (Publishers) Ltd.

Notes

1 Single Nucleotide Polymorphism – but don't let that spoil the story. SNP is usually said as 'snip'.

2 Shown Mills, Elizabeth. 2009. *Evidence Explained: Citing History Sources from Artifacts to Cyberspace*. 2nd edition, revised 2012. Baltimore, MD.: Genealogical Publishing Co. Inc.

3 Mantel, Hilary. 2017. The dead have something to tell us. *The Guardian*, Review p.2. Saturday 3 June 2017. From: Resurrection: The Art and Craft. *Reith Lectures*. BBC Radio 4, June 2017.

4 A grammatically odd term for a process, since it has no active component. Genealogical Proofing Standard, though quaint, would make more sense.

5 Board for Certification of Genealogists. 2014. *Genealogy Standards*. Nashville and New York: Ancestry.com.

6 Wrigley, E.A. ed. 1973. *Identifying People in the Past*. London: Edward Arnold (Publishers) Ltd.

7 Adams, Douglas. 1979. *The Hitchhiker's Guide to the Galaxy*. London: Pan. p. 3.

8 The Harvard Library website (http://guides.library.harvard.edu/cite/guides) recommends guides produced by other organisations such as the American Psychological Association and the Modern Language Association.

9 A third edition was published in 2017.

10 URLs in this book were accurate at the time of going to press, but may not work by the time you read this – that's the web for you.

11 Library of Congress Names. http://id.loc.gov/authorities/names.html.

12 Chicago Editorial Staff. 2010. *The Chicago Manual of Style: The Essential Guide for Writers, Editors and Publishers*, 16th ed. Chicago: University of Chicago Press. p. 657.

13 Started off by Ted Codd. If you must pursue it, his first paper on the subject was: Codd, E.F. 1970. A relational model of data for large shared data banks, *Communications of the ACM*. 13(6), pp. 377–387. doi:10.1145/362384.362685.

14 In the form of an entity-relationship diagram but, like normalisation, that is much too boring to go into.

15 Szucs, Loretto Dennis and Sandra Hargreaves Luebking, eds. 2006. *The Source: a Guidebook to American Genealogy*. 3rd ed. Provo, UT: Ancestry.

16 This is an initiative in the UK for placing circular plaques on buildings to name and commemorate some notable person who once lived there.

17 Durie, Bruce. 2009. *Scottish Genealogy*. Stroud, Gloucestershire: The History Press.

18 Centre for Hearth Tax Research. 2011. *Hearth Tax Online: Householders in late 17th century England*. http://www.hearthtax.org.uk.

19 Shrimpton, Jayne. 2014. *Tracing Your Ancestors Through Family Photographs: A Complete Guide for Family and Local Historians*. Barnsley, Yorkshire: Pen & Sword Family History.

Index

American Psychological Association, 25
arms 95–6
artefacts 8
assumption 8, 14
audit trail 10, 51, 124, 135, 139

belt and braces 28, 61–2, 75
bibliographic punctuation 30
bibliography 31, 60, 130–2, 140–1
biographical 40–2
bishop's Transcript 9, 14, 67–8
blog 9, 29, 50–1
Board for Certification of Genealogists 16
book chapter 39, 132

Chicago Manual of Style 25, 30, 31, 34
Chinese whispers 14
citation 6, 10–2, 16, 24, 25, 34, 36, 48, 62, 122, 124, 129, 130, 132, 135
author–date 24–5
numeric 24, 129
conference 37, 45–6
court proceedings 18, 110

data 7–8, 10–11, 13, 15, 129–30, 134, 136, 137
date
accessed 34
census 76
copyright 33
publication 84
regnal 122
diary 8, 74
dictionary 9, 39–42
Digital Object Identifier (DOI) 29, 43
digitisation 17
directory 39, 59, 82–4
dissertation 46
DNA 7–8, 137–8

e-book 27, 49, 53–4
edward Mark 24
electoral
listing 59, 80–1, 104
poll book 80–1
register 81–2
roll 82
e-mail 49, 124, 137
encyclopaedia 9, 39–40
endnote 11, 30, 129–31
e-referencing 53
EThOS 47
event 8–10, 14, 32, 57, 62, 74, 119, 123
evidence 8, 13–6, 34, 68, 80, 108, 114, 125, 137, 139

Facebook 50, 137
fact 5, 8, 10, 11, 13, 15–6, 20, 23, 56, 60, 111, 130, 133, 139
family bible 8, 74
feudal system 97, 102
footnote 11, 30, 129–31

genealogical
acceptability 16, 20
conclusions 6–7, 12–3, 16, 231, 139
date, 32–3
investigation 5, 7, 17, 24, 57, 63, 115, 132, 1355,
material 17–24, 27, 33–4, 47, 49, 57, 97,
practice 5–6, 25, 47, 50, 64, 78, 130, 139
proof Standard 16
reliability 8, 13–5, 20, 21, 34, 78, 124, 125
replicability 7
software 13, 23, 133
genealogy courses 5–6, 35, 50
GIGO 7, 134
GROS 62, 64, 77

Harleian Society 37–8
Harvard style 24–5, 30, 130, 133

image
digital 18–9
photographic 8, 39, 93, 125–6
record 65, 74, 77, 78
index 60–2
information 7–8, 136–7

journal 21, 43–5

land records
griffith's valuations 105
inquisitions post–mortem 100–1
manorial 97, 99
retours 102–3
royal charters 103–4
sasines 101
tithe apportionments and applotments 98, 105, 128
valuations 104, 105
letters 8, 47
library
Anglia Ruskin Library 26
British Library 47
Goldsmiths' Company Library 118
Library and Archives Canada 72
Library and Museum of Freemasonry 85
Library of Congress 31
National Library of Scotland 52, 128
National Library of Wales 90
Niagara Falls Public Library 72
Royal College of Surgeons Library 85
Society of Genealogists

Library 67
life event 42, 55, 58, 60, 76, 94, 117, 135–7
LinkedIn 50, 137
Linnaeus 56–7

maps 52, 56, 98–9, 127–8
marriage bond 68
Master of Science 5
Modern Language Association 25
monograph 30, 33, 37, 38, 52, 53, 83, 91, 120, 124
monumental inscriptions 59–60, 73, 91–3

Name Authority File 31
National Archives (Great Britain) 31, 34, 53, 65, 70, 97, 99
National Archives of Ireland 79
National Records of Scotland 64, 104, 105
newspaper 8, 9, 28, 56, 59, 60, 73, 94–5, 119, 132
non–conformist 58, 63, 65, 70
not proven 16

online forum 50
Oxford Dictionary of National Biography 9, 29, 42

paraphrase 10, 11
permalink 29, 90
plagiarism 12–3
poll book 80–1
poor relief 114–5
protocol book 91, 101

quotation 10–12, 45, 122

record linkage 16, 39
records

genealogical 55, 74
legislative 8, 121–2
material 57, 97–107
nominal 16, 18, 39, 57–9, 63–6
non–standard 56, 59, 117
procedural 57, 108–116
taxation 115
travel 108–110
vital 58, 63, 74, 94, 135
Register of Corrected Entries 59, 68
Register of Qualified Genealogists 6, 50, 85, 126
registration district 63–4, 75, 77, 78
research notes 23

SNP 7, 137
social media 136–7
source
authored narrative 14
collection 22, 28, 33–4, 61–2
date accessed 34
derivative 14
derived 14, 84, 90
derived primary 9, 14
edition 22, 33–7, 41
location 17, 21–2, 75, 117, 125, 127
material 9, 21, 74, 109
original 37, 60, 64, 75, 109, 113
primary 8–9, 14–5, 20–2, 24–5, 41, 47, 56, 60, 74, 95, 125, 131, 133–4
secondary 8–9, 13, 15, 20, 24, 30–48, 130, 132, 133
versions 22, 33, 35, 37, 45, 47, 53
volumes 30, 33, 35, 37–8, 43, 62–3
source category 57–8

material 57, 97–107
nominal 57, 63–96
procedural 57, 108–16
source type 26, 58–62, 117, 131
status animarum 75
superscript number 11, 24, 129–30
Surtees Society 37–8
systematic genealogy 5

terrier 99
thesis 46
tithe
applotments 105
apportionments 98, 104
maps 98, 128
transcript 9, 14, 60–2, 66–70, 78–9, 91–2
Twitter 9, 137

undertaker 69, 95
university
Anglia Ruskin 26
Harvard 24
Strathclyde 5–6, 24, 35
Dundee 35
URL
DOI 23, 29, 43, 45
fixed 43–4, 67, 78, 79
generic 28, 50, 53, 66

valuation roll 104–5
video 19, 50, 125–6
vlog 50–1

Wayback Machine, 34
web page 27–9, 33, 34, 49, 51–2
website 8, 9, 27–9, 32, 35, 41, 44, 51, 52, 56, 69, 90, 93, 99, 126, 138

YouTube 19, 126, 137